GRANDPA RULES

GRANDPA RULES

Notes on Grandfatherhood, the World's Best Job

Michael Milligan

Illustrations by Renee Reeser Zelnick

FALL RIVER PRESS

This 2009 edition published by Fall River Press,
by arrangement with Skyhorse Publishing.

Fall River Press
122 Fifth Avenue
New York, NY 10011

ISBN: 978-1-4351-2457-8

Printed and bound in China

10 9 8 7 6 5 4 3 2 1

To Jill, my spectacular and exquisite inspiration.
For everything. And so much more.

CONTENTS

FOREWORD

Before you dig into Mike Milligan's delightfully entertaining book, *Grandpa Rules*, there are a few things you should know. First, Mike is a very funny writer. Second, his loving and unique take on the wonderful world of grandfatherhood will bring smiles—and, at times, outright laughter—to grandfathers of all ages. And third, Mike promised that if I wrote something nice, he would stop pestering me.

As a proud and loving grandfather myself, I am learning that when my grandchildren visit, I immediately become their oldest stuffed bear and lumpiest trampoline. And as my grandchildren grow, I'll have Mike's book to tell me what to expect next.

So, fellow grandpas, try to remember where you left your pair of 99 Cent Store eyeglasses, grab that pint of ice cream you stashed in the basement freezer for whenever your wife or internist are not around, and sit down and enjoy *Grandpa Rules*.

Happy grandfathering, and remember to deposit the empty ice cream carton in the trash can outside. And do not put the spoon in the dishwasher. Wives notice things like that.

—**Bill Cosby**
August 2007

ON SALE NOW
7 Habits of Highly Effective GRANDMOTHERS
I ♥ gramma
Grandma moses
the grandma guide
the grandma guide
grandma's chicken soup
grandma's chicken soup
GoGo grandma

PREFACE

As I prepared for parenthood many years ago, I was lean, I was clean, I could remember why I walked from one room into another. And when I became a father for the first time, I had all sorts of guidance to help me in my new role of parenting. First, I could take important life lessons from my father and pass them on to my own children—mysterious pearls from his generation like "Avoid any job where you have to wear a name tag." And "Never drive behind a man with a hat on!"

Or, if I needed guidance that was actually understandable and remotely useful, there were thousands of books offering parenting advice. And if I chose to ignore that advice, I could still use those books to smack my little devils upside the head every so often to get their attention.

But when I learned I would soon be a grandfather, I was surprised to find that there were absolutely no books to help me through this new phase of my life. Oh, sure, there were shelves of books dedicated to grand*mothers*—all with cuddly covers depicting colorful spring bouquets or gentle little lambs.

But there was not a single book jacket that featured a sixty-four-year-old grandfather—napping in a Barcalounger with a cup holder big enough to accommodate a martini shaker—wearing an AC/DC T-shirt that stopped covering his stomach about twelve years earlier.

Then it struck me that there must be countless other grandfathers out there who were experiencing this same feeling of neglect.

Consider this: According to the U.S. Census of 1980—a year when I was in my prime as a father—the population of the United States was 240,132,887.

Today it is 296,496,649, an increase of over 56 million people. This only proves what many of us already know: That we are living longer—no matter what our children have done to shave years off our lives.

It also means that a lot of us are grandfathers, or about to become one.

Another telling statistic is that the United States' current adult population is approximately fifty-one percent female, which suggests that women outlive men. There are probably many scientific explanations for this, but I suspect that somehow a wife adds a few weeks to her life every time she says to her husband, "Don't you think it's time you bought some new undershorts?"

After studying this data, I set out to determine exactly how many grandfathers there are in the United States today. Using my extensive math and statistical talents, and after painstakingly checking and double-checking all my calculations, I can confidently estimate that there are somewhere between 1,827 and 28,382,036 (±3%) of us. I realize this number is a bit broad; I could have been much more precise if my computer were working properly. But my grandchildren visited this past weekend and used the keyboard to "play office," and now my desktop is covered with peanut butter and jelly, and my computer will only communicate in Cantonese.

So welcome to my world. In my happy career as a grandfather, I've discovered some universal truths that apply to grandfathers everywhere, and I consider it my pleasure to pass them on to you. For example, I've learned to take it in stride should I hear one of my grandchildren say, "Grandpa sure dresses funny." That's certainly a whole lot better than the child saying, "*Grandma* sure dresses funny; you should have seen what she wore to Grandpa's funeral."

So whether you're a fellow grandpa or a grandfather-in-waiting, I hope this book will guide you as you travel down the road of grandfatherhood.

Because, to borrow a phrase from back in the day … it's a real trip.

ONE

A GRANDPA? ME?

Yes, you. Because if you're reading this, odds are that you're already a grandfather. Or shuffling your way toward becoming one.

It's also likely that you're a member of the wonderful American generation whose mantra was "Think Young!" Well forty years later, we can *think* whatever we want; but the truth is that we've got more hard miles on us than a '64 Corvair.

And we're leaking oil just as fast.

Where did the years go? What happened to the age of "Sex, Drugs, and Rock and Roll"?

I think I know. We spent a lot of time raising our children and warning them not to do what we did—most of which we never came close to doing, because if we had, we'd likely be deceased, incarcerated, or living on a Maui mountaintop with my high school friend, Boomer, as he awaits the return of the Lizard King.

And while we were busy with parenting and work, somehow our lives went from Howdy Doody to jury duty.

From McCarthy hearings to hard-of-hearing.

From hi-fi to Wi-Fi.

And though it may hit you like an Ali forearm shiver, it's time to accept that you're actually old enough to be someone's *grandfather.* But how can that be? You dreamed of staying young forever!

Sadly, all of our dreams do not come true. If they did, there would be no more death. There would be no more hunger. There would be no more Michael Bolton albums.

Since becoming a grandfather, I've found it to be unbelievably fulfilling. But I never thought I'd actually *look* like a grandfather. And the first time I had to face that, it was about as fulfilling as a "very special episode" of *My Mother the Car.*

It happened while my wife, Jill, and I were visiting our grandchildren out of town and attending our five-year-old granddaughter's soccer game. Now I don't know about you, but when I was growing up in the fifties and sixties, soccer was not the hugely popular sport it is today, even in Los Angeles. And it certainly wasn't played on manicured suburban fields by perfectly-uniformed, cute granddaughters named Samantha. Rather, it was played on rough-hewn, bottle-strewn lots by prematurely mature fifteen-year-olds with names like Rico and Alfredo who sported moustaches, sleeveless T-shirts, and exotic-looking girlfriends—all of whom were certainly more physically blessed than any of the girls in my tenth grade class.

Except for maybe Joanie Beroni, who had already flunked two grades and who, in three years, would be skating with roller derby's New Jersey Devils.

But back to my granddaughter's game. As I stood on the sidelines with parents of her teammates, a pleasant, outgoing young mother of one of the girls approached and introduced herself.

"Hi," she said perkily. "I'm Christmas's mom."

"*Christmas*," I said, trying to hide my amusement. "What a nice name."

"Yes!" she chirped. "We named her after the most wonderful day of the year."

If I had done that, my oldest son's name would be *July Twelfth*, which—at the age of thirty-one—was the date he finally moved out of the house and into his own apartment.

"Nice to meet you," I said. "I'm Samantha's grandfather."

Like any deluded fifty-five-year-old man who looks in the mirror and sees a thirty-five-year-old stud, I anticipated what would happen next. When Mrs. Christmas heard that I was a grandfather, she would quite likely faint. When she came to, her eyes would grow wide with admiration as she checked out my perfectly understated hoop earring and my slightly graying—yet stylishly shaggy—hair.

"Her *grandfather*?" she'd say. "You're kidding! You don't look old enough to be Sami's grandfather. Her older brother, sure. Or maybe even an uncle. But grandfather? No way!"

"So totally way!" I'd respond, proving that I was as youthful as I looked.

So imagine my shock when Mrs. Christmas didn't come close to fainting … or tweak my earring … or even blink an eye. Instead, she turned to her husband, who was sitting nearby, eating a veggie wrap. "Adam," she barked, "this is Sami's grandfather. Get up and give him your chair. He won't be able to stand for the whole game."

And that was that.

To this suddenly irritating young woman, it was crystal clear that I was old enough to be someone's grandfather.

Later, when I learned that this incredibly insensitive soccer mom was thirty, I wanted to run up to her and say, "Thirty? Let me tell you something, Mrs. Christmas lady: You look at least thirty-two … and a *hard* thirty-two at that! I got ten bucks that says by the time you're fifty, you'll be sagging so badly that you'll try to sue the city for building the sidewalk too close to your breasts!"

All in all, I think I took it pretty well.

★ ★ ★ ★ ★

I tossed and turned in bed that night, and Jill sensed something was not right. "What's bothering you?" she asked.

I sighed. "I can't sleep," I said.

"I knew it," she said. "You snuck those last two taquitos, didn't you?"

"Well, yeah, but..."

"Great," she snapped, getting out of bed and opening all the windows.

After she kissed my forehead and dozed off, I thought back to my own grandfather, a loveable old man who wore a little hat with a feather and plaid Bermuda shorts with calf-high dark socks. A man who said things like "Judas Priest!" "Holy Moses!" and "Yessiree, Bob."

Could I have come to that?

When I finally found sleep, I had a very weird dream. It was 1958 and I was eleven years old. I was rotary-dialing my grandparents' phone number. But I soon realized that in my dream, my grandfather of 1958 had become a "Think Young" grandpa of 2008.

"Hi, Grandma. Is Grandpa home?" I asked when my grandmother answered the phone.

"No, honey, he's working out."

"Oh, in the garage?" I asked. After he retired, my grandfather had turned his garage into a woodworking shop with a lathe, power saws, and other sharp tools. As a result, Grandpa had a living room full of beautiful custom-made wooden furniture, a den with impressive mahogany shelves, and two fingers lopped off at the first knuckle.

Then, in my dream, my grandmother said something very strange.

"No, sweetie. Grandpa's not working out in the garage. He's at the gym."

"The *what*?" I asked.

"The gym. He's working out at the gym."

I couldn't believe what I was hearing. Back in 1958, there weren't gyms on every corner like today. There were only one or two per city, usually located in gritty sections of downtown and sandwiched between a transmission shop and the local bail bondsman. And in those days, there were only two types of people who went into these gyms: boxers whose ears had been slapped into the size of cantaloupes, and tanned and oiled bodybuilders—"weirdos in Speedos," my father called them.

Could it be that my grandfather, sixty-three years old and a lifetime smoker, was about to take up a career in the ring? If so, would he wear plaid Bermuda boxing shorts? And how would they tape his hands with his missing fingertips?

"The gym?" I repeated numbly to my grandmother in my dream.

"Yes," she said with a laugh. "Your grandpa wants to tone up his abs."

Abs? My seven-year-old dream mind wondered if that was what old people called the skin that dangled from their upper arms. Is that where old people kept their muscles?

"When will he be back?" I asked. This was an important phone call; I'd told my dad I needed a new transistor radio to listen to the World Series at school, and he asked me if I thought money grew on trees. What a dumb question, I thought; of course money doesn't grow on trees. It grows in Grandpa's wallet.

"He won't be home for a while," my grandmother said. "After the gym, he's stopping at the spa for a facial, manicure, and pedicure."

What?! I didn't know what those first two words were, but a *pedicure*?! I was almost positive that's the same word my parents used last week about that odd, fifty-year-old ex-priest who lived with his mother two blocks away, and who always wanted to play tag with the neighborhood kids until the police gave him a nice ankle bracelet to wear.

"I'll have Grandpa call you when he gets home," my grandmother said. "Or would you rather he text message you?"

"Do *what*?"

"Never mind. Now, if there's nothing else, sweetie, I have to go," said granny, as my dream got even weirder. "I'm off to have a boob job. See you at Christmas!"

That image jolted me awake, and it was then that I realized I needed help with this "grandfather thing."

So let this frightening dream be a lesson to you: At your age, never, ever have more than one taquito before bedtime.

TWO

UNPLANNED GRANDPARENTHOOD

Like many parents, the most life-changing decision I ever made was to have children. The *second* most important decision—once I'd had my kids and gotten to know them—was agreeing to keep them. If children are gifts, how come no one would accept mine when I tried to give them away?

But since we bring our children into the world, we are duty-bound to love them and nurture them and hope that they become responsible and caring adults. It's also important that we provide them with an education that will enable them to accomplish great things, like the ability to read "Apartments for Rent" ads in far-away newspapers before they reach Social Security age.

But you'll find that becoming a grandfather is different. It's not something you have a direct hand in, or worry about, or even think about when you wake up in the middle of the night. I know that when *I* wake up in the middle of the night, my only thought is, "Where did I put the bathroom?"

Since I had no say-so about becoming a grandfather, it only makes sense that I didn't get a vote about the things that began happening as our grandchild's arrival date drew nearer. Even though the soon-to-be-parents lived in their own house three hours away, things began changing in *my*

Z z z

house. These changes will also happen to *your* house, and when they do, remember that although your name appears on the property deed, you will have very little control over them.

First, don't be surprised if, when your daughter reaches her third month of pregnancy, she calls at least three times per hour to give you progress updates. You should also know that your wife will start doing strange things as well. You see, at my house, Jill hates answering the phone. But with a pregnant daughter, she could flatten five of Snoop Dogg's toughest bodyguards to grab the phone by the second ring.

As soon as she'd hear Dee's voice, Jill would gesture to me and point to our extension phone, indicating that I should immediately pick up and listen in so as not to miss a single word of the report. Like most husbands, I am invited to join this sort of phone conversation with my ears only. Should I make the mistake of actually saying anything, I'm met with, "Shhhh, I can't hear!"

"Hi, sweetie," Jill said.

"Hey, Mom. How are you guys doin'?"

"We're fine," Jill claimed, speaking for both of us.

But when Jill said we both were "fine," she was only telling *half* the truth—which is that *she* feels fine because she'd had a nice afternoon nap—while I, a man rapidly nearing grandfather age, am inexplicably forbidden from taking naps, even if I've been forced to listen to John Tesh's music after running a marathon … uphill.

In fact, just a few hours before this phone call from Dee, I was sitting in my favorite chair, reading the newspaper and still adjusting to the beautiful silence that moved into the house when the children moved out. And while I was enjoying the sports page, Jill bounded down the stairs, looking refreshed.

"Hello, sweetheart," I said. "How was your nap?"

I've noticed that the word "nap" can change a normally pleasant and lovely wife into something evil. It can cause her neck veins to bulge, her mouth to tighten, and her nose to shoot a stream of hateful fire at you.

"Nap?" Jill hissed as her head made a complete 360. "What makes you think I was taking a nap?!"

I paused. "Well..."

She glared.

"I went up to the bedroom to find my glasses..."

"And?"

"And I saw you lying on the bed."

"So?"

"So, your eyes were closed, you were making a noise just like the dog makes when he's sleeping, and there was just a little bit of drool coming from the side of your mouth. I put it all together."

Her eyes became scary, bright red circles. If you're a long-time husband, you already know this sign: Your wife is about to say something that should not be forgotten.

"Nice try, Clouseau, but I was *not* taking a nap!" Jill said. "I was resting my eyes."

"Oh," I said, smugly. "Well, what about yesterday when I dozed off and you woke me because I was taking a nap? What's the difference?"

"*What's the difference*?" she sputtered. "*You* were on the sofa in the den. Anyone could just walk right in and see you there with your mouth wide open."

Unless our home had also become our city's bus station, I wondered who would be walking through my den in the middle of the afternoon. It's just the two of us since the children moved away. And it couldn't be one of them, because I changed the security code before they hit the end of the driveway.

Then I recalled an animal program I had seen about lions. Husband lions have the right idea; they just lay around all day while the wife goes out for food. It's good to be King of the Jungle. Not Queen of the Jungle, or Prince of the Jungle. The King—a guy who can go out in public no matter how goofy his hair looks. And what brave deeds must the husband lion perform to warrant being King? Well, every once in a while he must roar to warn beasts—and noisy children—not to fool with him. I imagined how the King would feel if a lioness treated her husband in the same manner as her human counterpart.

The wife lion comes home, dragging dinner behind her, only to find her husband fast asleep in his lion's den.

"Hey, Mr. Big Time King, wake up!" she growls, scratching him and then biting his leg for good measure. "What do you think you're doing?"

"I was, uh, listening to the news coming over the jungle drums," says the husband lion, covering a yawn.

"You were taking a nap!"

"I wasn't taking a nap," he says. "I was resting my eyes."

"No, you were taking a nap!" she insists. "I saw you! And I'll bet everyone else saw you, too!"

"Everyone else? Like who?"

"The hyenas for starters. Hear them laughing? They probably walked by and saw you snoring with your mouth wide open."

"Okay, sweetie," the lion confesses. "Maybe I was having a catnap. Sorry."

"All right," she says, dropping supper at his paws. "But if it happens one more time, you're going out to catch your own wildebeest."

★ ★ ★ ★ ★

Back on the telephone, Jill asked, "How are *you* feeling, honey?"

"Amazing," Dee said. "This pregnancy thing soooooo agrees with me. I want to have six or maybe even seven."

As I covered the mouthpiece to hide my laughter, Dee mentioned that she felt the baby kick today. "I think we may have a punter. Or a Rockette," she said.

I thought about that, and since a Rockette has a guaranteed job for only three freezing weeks a year, I hoped for a punter.

The conversation continued for nearly an hour, but I quietly logged off when the ladies started discussing whether the motif of the baby's room should be early Bert and Ernie or retro Winnie the Pooh.

I recall another "update" three months later, when Dee was entering her eighth month of pregnancy. The temperature in her town had been over 100 degrees for so long that she and her husband were considering a move to someplace cooler—a corrugated metal duplex in Death Valley.

When the phone rang, I answered because Jill was out in the garage, antiquing a layette for the baby.

"Oh, hi, Dee," I said. "How are you feeling?"

"Feeling?!" she screamed. Suddenly, Mrs. Loves-to-Have-Babies had turned into Pregzilla. "My back hurts more than a Russian power lifter's. My hair has all the body of a Raggedy Ann doll; my emotions go from happy, to sad, to euphoric, to panic-stricken—all within ten exhilarating minutes! And don't tell me that I have that special glow. If I wanted a glow, I'd go to a tanning booth! I'm bigger than a manatee; I'm retaining more water than the Hoover Dam; and I need a forklift just to get out of the chair! How do you think I'm feeling?!"

Fortunately, my years of parenting had taught me exactly what to do in this situation.

I yelled out to the garage, "Jill, it's for you!"

But what if you're the father of a son who's about to become a father himself? Expect the phone calls to be far less frequent. And more general in nature.

"Hey! Everything all right?" you ask when he calls.

"Yeah."

"And my favorite daughter-in-law is feeling good?"

"Yeah."

"Good."

"Yeah."

Then there's silence. You know that he wants to talk to you about something, but you also know that speech was his least favorite subject in high school.

"Did you call to say something other than *yeah*?"

"Yeah. See, Dad, I went out to one of those furniture warehouses today and bought a crib, but when I got it home, all the assembly instructions were in Swedish. I could use some help putting it together."

"No problem," you say confidently, proud of him for acknowledging he needs help to do the job right.

"Honey, it's for you," you call, holding the phone out for your wife.

That night in bed when I put my arm around Jill, I was hit with a disconcerting thought. "It's gonna be weird," I said. "I've never slept with a grandma before."

"Keep talking like that, old man, and you never will," she said with a laugh. Then she kissed me and drifted off into a grandmother's dreams of bassinets and mobiles.

"Old man, hmm?" I thought. Maybe she's got a point. After all, I wasn't exactly "young." And whether I liked it or not, most people under twenty-five think that anyone who doesn't have an iPhone must've fought alongside Davy Crockett.

But "old man?"

Then, the more I thought about it, I realized this whole thing might have a huge upside.

I mean, what kind of wife would refuse an old man a decent nap?

THREE

THINGS THAT GO BEEP IN THE NIGHT

There was another change in our house that indicated the big day was drawing near: My loving wife, the soon-to-be grandmother who believes that cell phones are technology's way of interrupting valuable family time, began wearing a pager.

She took it with her everywhere, which meant her pager went to much nicer places than I did.

And because it was intended for emergency use only, I, of course, was not allowed to have the number.

"But what if I'm trimming the hedge in the yard and the clippers slip and I cut off both of my legs? Isn't that an emergency?" I asked.

"You doing yard work is not an emergency," she informed me. "It's a miracle."

And then, one night … BEEP!

I tried to wake up as quickly as possible. But in the time it took me to pry my eyes open, Jill had somehow managed to shower, dress, and visit her hairdresser.

"Get up!" she said. "It's time!"

"Time for what?" I mumbled, trying to clear the cobwebs.

"The baby's coming!"

"Here?"

"Will you please wake up? The kids are leaving for the hospital."

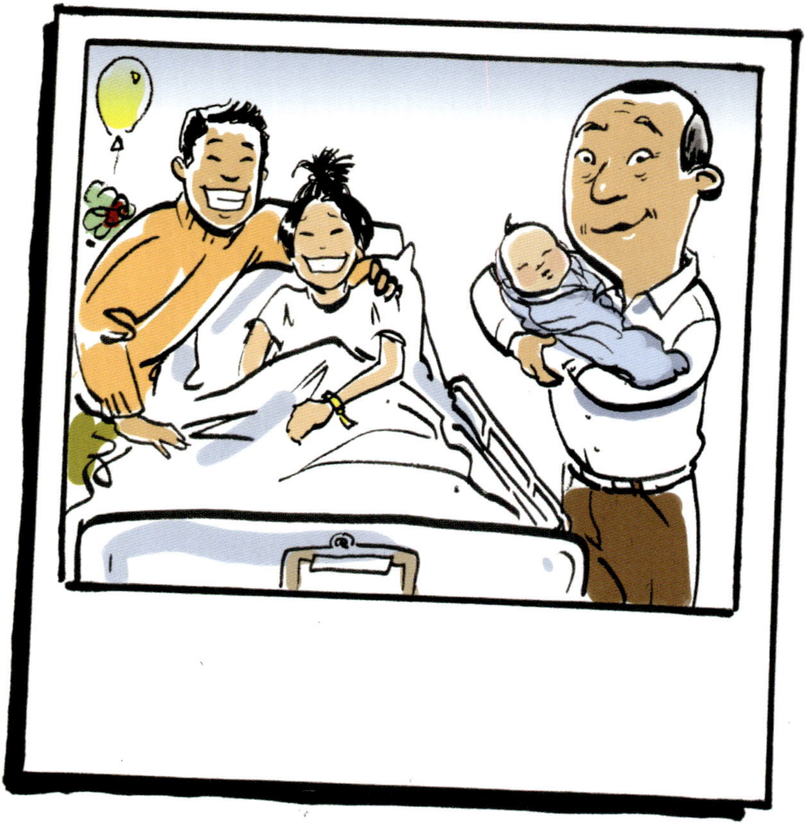

"Maybe it's false labor," I suggested, hoping for a few more hours of sleep, since I'm not allowed to nap.

"No, it's the real thing. Look."

She showed me her beeper.

"See? *9-9-9*!" she said.

"What does *that* mean?" I asked, fighting to separate my lips and wondering who had put the glue on them while I was sleeping.

"It means," she said matter-of-factly, "that Dee's contractions are thirty minutes apart."

As I stumbled out of bed, I asked why 9-9-9 represents *30* minutes. Why not *30-30-30?*

"It's our special code," she explained in a way that only wives can explain. Simply put, she meant that the code should be obvious to any idiot.

Any idiot, that is, except me.

And as I reached for my most comfortable clothes, I imagined a foreign spy submarine submerged just off the coast of Santa Monica.

"9-9-9," says the head spy. "What do you think that means?"

"It's some kind of complicated code," says the assistant spy. "Darn! I believe those women have outsmarted us again. We'll never find out when that child is going to be born."

"Okay, I'm ready to go," I told her.

As I started out, she looked at my outfit. "You're actually going to wear that old sweat suit?"

I looked at the clock on the nightstand. I was not aware the hospital had a dress code, particularly at 4:30 a.m., which is about when we'd arrive after our 300-mile drive.

"No one's going to see me," I explained.

"Our *grandchild* will. And do you want that to be the first thing she sees you in?"

I explained that I had read somewhere that babies don't have clear vision until they're two or three days old. I suspect that this is nature's way of shielding their new eyes from old people who squint at them while saying things like "wooo-baaa-bee-bee" in a falsetto that only Tiny Tim would appreciate. Because if newborns were forced to see such things, they could grow up to be chain smokers or even waffle iron repairmen. Or both.

And with that, I defiantly strode toward the door, wearing my comfortable old sweat suit. I'm as nice as the next guy, but sometimes a man has to put his foot down, even if it's wearing an old slipper.

When we hurried into the hospital about five hours later, the slacks and shirt that Jill dressed me in still looked fresh, even after the long drive. When I asked an orderly for directions to the maternity ward, he checked my attire and said, "I'll take you there myself, doc."

We arrived as they were wheeling Dee toward the delivery room. She wasn't particularly happy, but seemed to be doing much better than her husband, who looked like a man who had just consumed a gallon of very bad clam dip on a very hot day. Jill ran to Dee's side and kissed her.

"Don't worry, honey. Everything will be fine."

"That's right," I said, patting her hand. "Good luck, love. I'll see you when you're a mom."

"Wait a minute," the father-to-be said to me. "You're not going in to see it?" I immediately recognized this as a case of misery loving company.

"No, Ron, I'm not."

"How come?"

I wanted to tell him that there are two things a man does not want to see: His daughter in pain, and his daughter in stirrups.

Plus, I was dressed too nicely.

But instead, I said "because it's something a husband and wife should share together."

"But *Jill*'s going to be in there," he said as a nurse handed him a gown and mask.

And there it was: my first glimpse into one of the many differences between grandmothers and grandfathers.

When the chips are down, grandmothers can be counted on to do whatever's necessary.

When the chips are down for grandfathers, we just go into the kitchen and get more chips.

I spent the next forty-five minutes pacing and perspiring and wishing I'd worn my old sweat suit. Then Jill came out of the delivery room, and when she removed her mask, I could see her big smile.

She ran into my arms and all she could say through her tears was, "She's beautiful."

A little while later we went in to visit the new mother.

"How do you feel?" I asked Dee.

"Amazing! What an incredible experience!"

Incredible? This young woman had just gone through what is arguably the most painful and grueling of physical demands, and she describes it as "amazing"? Can this be the same person who once forged her mother's signature on a high school P.E. slip to get out of jogging one lap around the track because "she didn't want to smell gnarly"?

Soon a nurse came in with the baby. When Jill had said she was beautiful, I'd smiled politely because all fathers hear that when their own children our born. But in truth, most babies look more like newborn pterodactyls from *Jurassic Park* than human beings.

I've found that babies normally don't become "beautiful" until they're about two weeks old. And they stay beautiful until they're teenagers, when the only thing beautiful about them is that in a few short years you can ship them off to college.

But this child *was* absolutely beautiful. The most gorgeous child I had ever seen! Man, this grandfather thing was coming pretty easy to me.

Our son-in-law grabbed a camera and snapped a picture of me holding my new granddaughter.

Three days later, that picture was proudly posted on our refrigerator, where it has remained for the past thirteen years, and is now surrounded by pictures of our other grandchildren in various stages of growth and toothlessness.

And whenever I look at that particular picture, I'm able to recount every little detail of the day I first became a grandfather. And even after all this time, I still pat myself on the back, because—for such an important occasion—I stood firm and didn't let Jill talk me into wearing that ragged old sweat suit.

FOUR

WHO'S YOUR (GRAND)DADDY?

Unfortunately, U.S. divorce rates have more than doubled since 1950, so it follows that many babies born today will have more than two grandfathers, especially if these babies have grand*mothers* from the sixties who still wear tie-dye and use words like *groovy* and *bitchin'* to describe their latest tattoos.

Although many of my era came into the world with only two sets of grandparents, it's common for today's children to have family trees with the names of more grandfathers than the obituary page of the *Miami Herald*.

Of course, while many of today's new grandfathers will continue to have a direct biological link to their grandchildren, this is not an absolute necessity. There are other important qualities that help one qualify. These include:

- a willingness to watch the same singing starfish video so many times that you'd like to donate your corneas *before* you're dead;
- knowing the difference between Hannah Montana and Mona Arizona;
- and developing the ability to sleep in a bed while your three-year-old granddaughter thrashes, twists, turns, and digs her toes into areas of your body that you'd rather she didn't.

MOM BIRTHDAY
GRANDMA BIRTHDAY
GRANDPA BIRTHDAY
DAD BIRTHDAY
NICE OLD MAN SLEEPING WITH GRANDMA BIRTHDAY

And as the rate of multiple marriages continues to increase, I have discovered a new subculture of middle-aged men I call G.B.M.s (Grandfathers by Marriage).

The important thing to remember in all of this is that *grandfather* is more than a title. It's a feeling.

Let's say an older man marries a woman who already has college-age grandchildren. It's not likely that her grandchildren would suddenly begin calling him "Grandpa." Nor, I suspect, would the man truly *feel* like a grandfather to them. It's more likely they would call him "the nice old guy who's sleeping with Grandma." There is a problem with that, though: For his birthday, it would be very hard to find a greeting card with that title on it.

Now I'd like to tell you about my good friend, Pete. His nineteen-year marriage produced one child, a son whom he loved without reservation. But when his marriage ended, so did Pete's self-esteem, and other than visits with his son, he spent the next year living in a drab rental apartment and going out about as often as the Unabomber.

And whenever he needed cheering up, he'd rent a copy of *Kramer vs. Kramer.*

And as much as his friends tried, Pete declined countless invitations for dinner, movies and, of course, blind dates. But finally, Pete agreed to go with us to the wedding of a mutual friend's daughter, but only after receiving a call from the bride-to-be telling him than she couldn't think of a better wedding present than having him there.

Pete is known as a very thrifty man, and I've always wondered if this call got to him on an emotional level, or because it offered him a chance to save a hundred bucks and a trip to the mall where he might run into someone he knew.

In any event, Pete sat with us during the ceremony and only dabbed his eyes once … at the "till death do us part" part.

But as it turned out, those were the last tears Pete would shed for quite a while. Because during the reception, while Pete was alone at the bar sulking and nursing his third Shirley Temple, a woman named Lauren approached and ordered a Nancy Lopez. The bartender was stumped; and when Lauren explained that a Nancy Lopez was an Arnold Palmer with a dash of Tabasco, Pete couldn't help chuckling. That led Lauren to strike up a conversation and before long, the two of them discovered that they had an awful lot in common. Lauren, too, had recently come out of a long-term marriage and also had to be goaded into attending the wedding. They were about the same age. They each had one child—Lauren a daughter who was a year younger than Pete's son. What's more, they learned that they had both attended UCLA and were avid Bruins fans. And if that weren't enough, on the drive home, Pete giddily told us the ultimate coincidence: He *sold* books, and Lauren *read* books!

They began going out regularly, and have been blissfully wed for the past ten years. Lauren's daughter has also since married, and five years ago she called Pete and Lauren to announce that she was pregnant.

They were both thrilled at the news, with Pete being particularly happy for Lauren. He confessed to me that he was also a bit jealous, in that it wasn't his child who was having the baby. I reminded him that his son Jason was happily married and surely Pete would be receiving the same kind of phone call very soon.

(Note: As it turns out, "happily married" and "very soon" proved to be a bit optimistic, because Jason was divorced a short time later. Shattered by the experience, Jason has expressed no desire to re-marry or even seriously date, instead resigning himself, at age thirty-four, to spending the rest of his life living with his mother. This is unacceptable to Pete, who has put himself on Red Alert to find a young lady to help Jason out of his funk. In his sales job, Pete has met several perfect candidates, but Jason has dismissed each of them after only one date. So, recently, Pete has had to relax his standards for a prospective daughter-in-law, and will now consider any young lady so long as she has never worked for either the Mayflower Madam or Heidi Fleiss.)

From the outset of her pregnancy, Lauren's daughter affectionately began calling Pete "Grandpa," even though the baby would have two "real" grandfathers, both of whom were extremely good and decent men. Yet as much as everyone treated him like family, Pete couldn't help feeling like an outsider.

So I told Pete about my Uncle Leo, a really funny guy who was married to my Aunt Marie. Leo was far and away my favorite uncle, partly because whenever the family got together, my other uncles wore slacks and dress shirts, while Uncle Leo sported dark blue jeans and a T-shirt with rolled-up sleeves, which provided him an excellent storage area for his cigarettes.

My other uncles were nice enough, but they were always arguing politics with each other, whereas Uncle Leo preferred talking with me and, more surprisingly, listening to what I had to say. Uncle Leo and Aunt Marie had no children of their own, and I suspected that if Leo ever had a son, he'd want one like me.

Uncle Leo made his living as a handyman, and whenever he told his "fix-it" stories, he'd always let fly with a few "damns" and "sonofabitches." Then he'd wink at me, knowing that such language titillated my young Roman Catholic ears and irritated the hell out my parents, which I assumed was the reason they didn't seem to have the same affection for Uncle Leo that I did. I truly loved Leo, and was saddened when he and Aunt Marie moved to Ohio. I never saw him again, but I thought of him often … particularly when I saw a man with hard-pack Marlboros rolled up in his sleeve.

Years later, when I wanted invite Leo and Marie to my wedding, I couldn't understand my mother's resistance. "Of course Marie will come," she told me. "But not that Leo."

That Leo? What happened? Had they divorced? Had Leo died? Or worse, had he become a Democrat?

Finally Mom admitted the truth: Uncle Leo and Aunt Marie were never really married. They'd been "living in sin" all those years … until Leo ran off with "some trollop he met at a package store." My mother sighed. "He's not your real uncle, Mike. We just called him that to make him feel like family."

But after I thought about that for a while, I realized that it didn't matter who Leo was or wasn't married to—he was my favorite uncle, and nothing could change that. And I told Pete that if he could be as kind and loving and important to his grandchild as Leo was to me, then he would be a wonderful grandfather.

A *real* one.

Then came the big day: Lauren's granddaughter was born.

She and Pete were there for the birth, and soon went in to see the new mother and baby. That was when Lauren's daughter gently handed Pete the newborn with the instruction "Say hello to your granddaughter."

Pete later told me that when he stared into the baby's amazingly dark eyes, he thought a thousand thoughts about what wonderful things this child would bring to him and Lauren … and to all her grandparents. Then Pete realized that he had better hand the baby back to her mother and excuse himself.

He knew he was about to cry and he preferred to do it in private.

As Pete and Lauren's granddaughter has grown, it's obvious that this now rosy-cheeked four-year-old adores Pete. The child has proven over and over again that she loves him as her grandfather; hugs and kisses him as her grandfather; and asks him for money as her grandfather. And Pete knows there's no doubt about it … he's her grandfather.

★ ★ ★ ★ ★

A few years ago, Jill and I had just returned from a weekend visiting our grandkids, when my sister called to say that Leo had died.

The next evening, I landed in Cincinnati and made it to the funeral home just in time for Leo's Rosary, held the night before his burial Mass. Many people think that Catholics—particularly Irish ones—spread out the funeral process over two days so that they'll have an excuse to tip a few more.

Well, I can tell you that this is absolutely untrue.

We don't need an excuse.

Out in front after the Rosary, I learned that Leo had married "the trollop," and that they'd had two kids who were now parents themselves. And even in their grief, I could tell that they were a family of great joy.

As I stood there alone, a woman approached and asked me if I was related to Leo. I thought about that for a moment, then said, "I sure am. He was my uncle. My favorite one."

"Buh-Buh!"

FIVE

THE NAME GAME

At birth, the first thing we're given is a heartbeat. The second thing is a name. Some parents name their children after a family member or a friend. Some parents name their children after historical figures. And it seems that some of today's young parents name their children after too many Jägermeisters.

As the arrival of our grandchild drew near, we received regular calls from the soon-to-be parents, telling us the latest names they were considering for the baby.

"If it's a boy, we're thinking *LaSalle*; if it's a girl, *Nova*."

I wondered if they were giving birth to a child or a sedan. As I was about to suggest that the baby should have a mechanic instead of a pediatrician, Jill's look told me that if I said another word, it would be my final one.

But whatever the parents' selection process, one of the first things a baby learns—right after learning how to make such a big smell come from such a little body—is its name. Our youngest granddaughter is named Claire. She loves me, but if she's playing in her crib and I say, "Hello there, Steve," she will not respond. She may, however, think that I have forgotten to take my ginkgo biloba.

That's why a name is important; you grow up with it, secure that it will always be yours. No one can take it from you. You will have it until you go to your grave. Or until you become a grandfather … whichever comes first.

For those of you who are very new grandfathers, it's likely that you've spent more than a few hours thinking about what you'd like your grandchild to call you. Some of you may settle on the ever-popular "Grandpa Handsome." Others may opt for something a bit more subtle, like "Grandpa Favorite."

But before you give it any more thought, you need to pay close attention to what I am about to tell you.

You have no choice in the matter.

The baby will decide what to call you. So get used to the fact that your naming will be left to a creature whose greatest achievement has been sleeping through the night without pooping.

And whatever name your first grandchild gives you—no matter how foolish—it will continue to be your name for every grandchild that follows. When my oldest grandchild, Sydni, was about seven months old, she pointed at up me and gurgled what sounded to everyone like "Buh-Buh!"

"Did you hear that?" her mother cried out.

"She called you Buh-Buh!" her father said, patting me on the back with such excitement that you'd think the child had just recited the Gettysburg Address. In Latin. I, on the other hand, will never know what my beautiful granddaughter was trying to say that day. For all I know, "Buh-Buh" could have been her way of saying, "Hey, if you all think strained carrots are so tasty, why don't *you* eat them?"

But I had no choice in the matter, so for the rest of my life as a grandfather, I will be "Buh-Buh." I've grown to like it; and although it may lack pizzazz, it'd certainly garner me some attention should I ever start hanging with the NASCAR crowd.

But why "Buh-Buh"? What made those sounds come out of her mouth? While pondering this, I realized that an infant's "vocabulary" is limited by the sounds it can make. And this led me to one of my greatest grandfather discoveries to date:

THE BABY ALPHABET

Normally by the age of three or so, a child gains command of all twenty-six letters of the alphabet. Children will use all these letters until the age of thirteen, when they stop using the letter "g" at the end of "ing" words. They will continue this practice until they apply for their first real job, which should ideally occur before they reach the age of thirty-six.

I have observed that for the first year or so of a baby's life, its alphabet seems to consist of only eleven letters: A, B, D, E, I, M, N, O, P, T, and U. To prove this theory, all I had to do was observe Sydni cooing to herself in her crib.

"Tuh-muh-bee-duh-poe-tee-nuh," is what she mumbled as she saw me staring down at her. That can be loosely translated to mean, "When I get as old as that man, will I have hair in *my* nose?"

Vowels are easy for a baby because *a, e, i, o,* and *u* require very little tongue development. And as any parent knows, a child's tongue can only be fully developed by sticking it out at his brothers and sisters.

Some consonants are easy for babies, too. The easiest one for infants—and therefore the most popular—is the letter "M." This is probably why the first "word" many infants utter is "mama." It is also why their second word is usually *money.*

Other consonants, however, are much more difficult for them. Take the letter "K." There's just too much tongue/palate coordination required. So if you're expecting your grandchild to call you by your name and your name is Keokuk, you might want to go on vacation until the child begins shaving. Or get a legal name change.

To prove my point, let me tell you a story about my friend, Craig. Craig is a bear of a man; and I use the term "bear" literally, because several times Craig has broken into my refrigerator and eaten all my food. A former college football linebacker and retired policeman, Craig has spent a lifetime holding his own against the biggest and baddest around. But as a father and grandfather, he is the gentlest, kindest, most nurturing man since Mister Rogers. But Mister Rogers sang better and looked a lot nicer in a cardigan.

Craig visited his new grandson daily. He'd gently hold the infant in his burly arms and say, "Hi, little man. I'm your Grandpa Craig. Can you say *Grandpa Craig*?" Most of the time, the child would stare at him and burp. Other times the baby would suddenly begin kicking his legs and jerking his arms spasmodically, like an overturned turtle. But never, ever did the baby say "Grandpa Craig." Or anything even close to it.

But then one day, there was an apparent breakthrough. After visiting his grandson, Craig came over to our house, thrilled. In fact, he was so excited that he constructed and downed *two* Reuben sandwiches.

"Okay," he said, explaining his joy, "I'm holding the baby like I always do and I say, 'Can you say "Grandpa Craig"?' And you know what he did? He looked right at me and said *mee-dah*!"

Mee-dah?

"And it was clear as a bell, too! Swear to God! The kid's almost got it!"

I looked at Craig and feared that an overdose of sauerkraut and spicy mustard was causing frontal lobe gastritis.

When I told him that I didn't see the connection, Craig was dumbfounded by my lack of vision.

"Don't you see? *'Grandpa Craig? Mee-dah?'* We're definitely on the right track. I'm beginning to think the kid might be a genius."

Maybe so, but the little genius never uttered those two syllables again.

Craig was crestfallen until several weeks later, when he answered the phone at home one evening.

On the line, a strange female voice said, "Tay-Tay?"

Craig wondered what poor fool would have a name like that.

"Tay-Tay? Sorry, but there's no Tay-Tay here," Craig informed the caller.

"Oh, but I think there is," she said.

"No, I'm afraid you have the wrong number. Good night."

But before he could hang up, he heard, "Daddy, it's me!"

Craig realized it was his daughter, who had been speaking in that annoying baby talk we all used when we were new parents.

"He said it, Daddy! The baby said your name!"

Craig was thrilled. "He said 'Grandpa Craig'?"

"No," said his daughter. "*Tay-Tay*! That's what he calls you!"

(Note: I later explained to Grandpa Craig that in the baby alphabet, the difficult consonants "C" and "R" apparently became a "T," the easy "AY" sound stayed "AY," and that the child dropped the "G" at the end. So at least in this respect, his grandson was about twelve years ahead of his time.)

His daughter continued, "I held up your picture and said, 'Who's this, honey?' He looked at it and said, 'Tay-Tay.'"

"Really?" said Craig, on cloud nine.

"Really. And he did it three different times. Isn't that precious?"

And at that moment, it was "Good-bye, Craig; hello, Tay-Tay!"

The very next day, Craig went to the Department of Motor Vehicles to order personalized "TAY-TAY" license plates. Not surprisingly, they were still available.

And a week later, when the four of us went out to dinner, Craig and his wife approached the hostess about their reservation.

"Your name?" the hostess asked.

"Smith," said Craig's wife.

"No, it's under Tay-Tay," Craig said proudly.

Now, do you need you any further proof that becoming a grandfather can lead a grown man to do some wonderfully goofy things?

And it's not just Craig. For centuries, seemingly intelligent men have been putty in their grandchildren's chubby little hands.

There's a story—from Aeschylus I believe, or maybe it was Neil Simon (I always confuse the two)—about two grandfathers in ancient Greece who were known to their grandchildren as PoPo and Dah-Bee. One day, PoPo was out for a walk with his young grandson when he spotted Dah-Bee approaching with his grandchild. PoPo and Dah-Bee were fast friends who often whiled away lazy Athens afternoons debating such weighty topics as the finality of death, the efficacy of democracy, and the origins of the age-old conundrum *I know you are, but what am I?*

This day, the men stopped to talk, but before long their grandkids grew antsy and started giving each other wedgies. Finally, PoPo's grandson said to him, "I'm hungry, PoPo. Can we get stop at McBaklava's on the way home?"

Then the other little one said to his grandfather, "I want to go, too. And don't forget, Dah-Bee, we promised Grandma we'd pick up her toga at the cleaners. She gave you her ticket and told you not to lose it, remember?"

"Of course I remember," said Dah-Bee.

PoPo and Dah-Bee smiled at each other as Dah-Bee said to his friend, "See you tomorrow, Plato."

"You got it, Socrates," PoPo said, taking his grandson's hand and heading off to get something to eat.

After Socrates waved good-bye, he began searching his robes for his wife's laundry ticket. He knew he had it somewhere.

Happy Birthday Everyone!

SIX

RIGHT OFF THE SHOWROOM FLOOR

Of course, the biggest difference between having your own children and having grandchildren is one that brings the greatest joy to grandparents: You can love them. You can kiss them. And then, after you've spoiled them, you can send them back to where they came from.

I've found that a helpful way to fully understand the differences between your children and your grandchildren is to compare them to automobiles.

Your own children are like the family car.

Remember when you brought home your first new car? As soon as the neighbors saw you pull into your driveway, they came over to admire it.

"What a beauty," one said.

"Mmm, mmm," said another, taking a deep whiff. "There's nothing like the smell of a new one."

"Seeing yours makes me want to have one, too," said the neighbor who was always trying to keep up with the Joneses, even though the Joneses got divorced and moved far away two years ago.

These are the same things they said when you brought home your first child.

But as your child got older, the neighbors became less enamored with it, and sometimes wished that you'd trade it in for a newer, quieter one. Especially when it got to be about ten years old and started making funny noises that often resulted in unpleasant odors.

Just like your family car.

And several years later, when you brought another new one home, the neighbors hardly seemed to notice. And even though you got a new one, you and your wife decided to keep the older one as well, believing—in spite of all the evidence against it—that someday it might actually become a *classic*. And should that happen, all the time and money you spent on maintenance would be well worth it. As the years passed, whenever you brought home other new ones, you always hung on to your older ones, even though they had become increasingly expensive to maintain.

You provided them with regular check-ups, offered plenty of tender loving care, and tried to keep them clean. Yet no matter what you did, they seemed to drop off in performance the older they got. Eventually, you had to face the harsh reality that none of them was likely to become a classic. But because of their great sentimental value, you couldn't get rid of them. Sure, sometimes they went out for a test drive, but they always seemed to end up back at your house.

Your grandchildren, on the other hand, are fun new rental cars. Normally, you only have them for a few days, and when you first pick them up, they are clean, shiny, and full of gas. You will decline the extra insurance because you're experienced ... you know what you're doing. You tell the people who own the rental car not to worry ... you've been doing this since they were born!

But still, they'll give you pages of instructions before they'll let you take the car, and they'll insist on telling you what kind of fuel it takes and how often it takes it. They'll tell you what to do if it has an oil leak. They'll even give you an after-hours number to call in case of emergency.

Then the last thing they'll tell you is not to take the rental car to certain places.

That's when you and your wife smile, because now you know exactly where you're going first.

After all, what's so wrong with the car getting a little mud on it? You'll be returning it Sunday night, and if it's dirty, so what? It's not like they'll never rent you the car again.

So you spend the entire weekend taking the rental car places you haven't been in years.

You go to the beach, and get sand all over it.

You go to the amusement park, and get cotton candy all over it.

You go to the kiddy pizza place with the scary clown and get vomit all over it.

And of course you take it to visit all your friends, so they can see how lucky you are to have such a beautiful new model.

And then, after you and your wife have enjoyed enjoy a fun-filled, wonderful weekend with your beautiful rental, you get to return it. And even though you're both exhausted, your wife will insist on washing it before you drop it off.

And when you do, the rental car will look exactly like it did when you picked it up. You'll tell the rental agents how much you enjoyed every minute of the two days and how good the car was.

And as you go to sleep Sunday night, you try to remember every precious detail of your weekend so you can tell your co-workers all about it as soon as you walk into the office the next morning.

But when you try to get out of bed on Monday, you realize you won't be walking *anywhere* soon, unless your bed grows legs. This is because you've made the mistake that most grandparents make: After a hectic and fun-filled weekend with your rental car, you've fooled yourself into thinking that you can rebound just like you did when you were a teenager. But you are not a teenager. Unless you give your age in German Shepherd years.

Based on my experience, here's what will happen after your wild weekend with your rental car: When you realize your legs feel like wet linguine, you will turn to your wife for help. But she will be lying flat on her back, eyes wide open, blankly staring at the ceiling.

"Darling?" you say.

"Ungh," she mumbles.

"How do you feel?"

"Ungh."

"Is it like you've been hit by a convoy of lumber trucks?"

"Ungh."

"Then I don't suppose you could help me find my feet."

"Ungh."

It will take at least twenty minutes before your legs will start receiving commands from your brain. And when you're finally able to hobble toward the bathroom, you will do it with the help of your late mother-in-law's old walker that was folded under the bed. It's at times like these you're thankful that your wife never throws anything away. And when you look at the legs of the walker, you also solve the mystery of what happened to some of your old tennis balls.

After an hour in the bathroom, you make it to the phone and dial very carefully, because even the ends of your fingers are exhausted. You call your office and tell them you won't be in today.

"What's wrong? You really sound beat."

"Yeah. I think it's the flu or something. I had it all weekend."

"Really? Because Charlie here thought he saw you going into that crazy pizza place with your grandkid on Saturday."

There's only one thing you can say to that.

"Ungh."

"You be in tomorrow?"

"Ungh."

"Good. See you then. And feel better."

"Ungh."

Later that day, when you've made your way to the kitchen, you discover something that probably would have prevented you from getting to work on time, even if you *had* felt better that morning. When you put your dirty cereal bowl in the dishwasher, you spot your wallet on the bottom rack. Apparently your granddaughter decided that was a good place to store it when she was playing "ATM."

And later, you also discover that the bureau containing your undershorts has been mysteriously locked and you can't open it. Because the key you hid in a place where no one could possibly find it is missing.

This teaches you an important grandfather lesson: There is no hiding place that's safe from your grandkids. If we were serious about finding Osama bin Laden, we would just send out a posse of four-year-olds to hunt him down.

When Monday night rolls around, do not be concerned if you go to bed very early and fall asleep before the news.

The six o'clock news.

I've learned that it normally takes about forty-eight hours for a grandfather's body and mind to rebound from a fun-filled weekend with a rental car, and Wednesday night, you and your wife should be back to calling each other by your real names instead of your grandparent names, "Wah-Wee" and "Wah-Woo." Or, in our case, "Buh-Buh" and "Gaji."

By Thursday evening, things should be back to normal. You have a quiet dinner at home, just the two of you. There are no frozen waffles or macaroni and cheese in sight.

After dinner, you hold hands on the couch and talk about how this coming weekend you intend to relax and catch up on your reading. Maybe you'll even go to a movie that doesn't have any surfing penguins in it.

Then Friday afternoon your phone will ring. You will answer it and your daughter will tell you she has some great news. Her husband has to go to New York for a few days on business, and asked her to go with him.

At first she didn't think she could do it, but then she remembered how much fun you said you had with the grandbaby the past weekend, so why not try it again?

"Sure, honey, we'd love to," you say.

When you hang up, your wife sees the blank, vacant stare on your face. She asks what your daughter wanted.

When you answer with a numb "ungh," she gets the picture.

And the picture is drawn with crayons.

Five days later, you will go pick up your rental car once again.

But this time, you'll be sure to take the extra insurance.

SEVEN

DIFFERENT MUSCLES

Many of your grandfather friends will tell you that grandparenting involves an entirely different set of muscles from parenting.

Do not always believe what your friends tell you because they—like you—are old, and often have trouble distinguishing fact from fiction. Remember, these are the same friends who told you to dump your Microsoft shares, to never bet on the Red Sox, and that a colonoscopy can be a whole lot of fun.

The truth is, grandparenting and parenting take *exactly the same muscles*. Unfortunately, they are muscles that you gladly put into retirement when your youngest child stopped demanding piggyback rides at the age of eighteen.

Consider this:

When I ran the 100-yard dash in high school over forty years ago, I used my leg muscles for speed, my arm muscles for thrust and momentum, and my chest muscles to control my breathing. And often—as I approached the finish line—I would use my brain muscles to wonder, "Do they give a ribbon for finishing fifth?"

Today, the only way I could sprint 100 yards is if a bear or a rabid Scientologist were chasing me. Or a rabid Scientologist bear. I would also likely skedaddle if a magazine salesman knocked on my door and I recognized him as

one of my children. And since I can't move as fast as I used to, I'd probably end up with bear saliva on my backside and a lifetime subscription to *Field & Stream*. Still, I would've used exactly the same muscles I used back in high school. Just because I'm older, I would *not* have used my nose muscles to help me run. Or my tongue muscles to help me pump my arms. But I might have used my finger muscles to plug my ears so I didn't have to hear all about Tom and Katie's philosophies on child-rearing.

Because many grandfathers have forgotten what muscles and muscle groups they used as fathers, I'll go over some of them and compare how they are used in fatherhood versus grandfatherhood.

And remember, to young children, size *does* matter. But just because your waistline is twice the size it used to be, don't be fooled into thinking that you are twice as strong.

The Upper Arms and Shoulders

In fatherhood, these muscles were used for a wide variety of fun activities that usually began when your child was about nine months old. One of the most popular of these was taking your child under the arms and tossing him skyward. Then you'd watch as his eyes became as big as saucers and his arms opened reflexively, like a baby condor falling from his nest. He'd hold his breath, anticipating the rapid descent, and then would burst into uncontrollable and relieved laughter when you caught him. As a father, you were able to perform this move roughly forty-seven consecutive times, or until your child threw up on you.

In grandfatherhood, you will think that you can perform the same trick with your grandchild. But before you try, heed this warning: When you launch your grandchild upward, **DO NOT LET GO OF HIM!** Be sure to maintain constant contact with him on the way up and the way down.

There are a couple of important reasons for this.

First, if you toss him up while you're wearing your bifocals, you might see two of him, and catch the wrong one coming down. Second, if you throw the child so high that it takes a while for him to come down, you might forget what you did and walk away before he lands.

And unlike when you were younger, you'll only be able to perform four or five repetitions before you grab for your inhaler. You should not try to do more, unless you own stock in Advil or if you enjoy walking around for the next two weeks feeling like you have a flaming javelin stuck in your shoulder.

The Lower Back

Throughout fatherhood, these muscles were among the most important and useful muscles you possessed. It was the lower back that allowed a father to lean over a crib and kiss his beautiful baby good-night. It was also these muscles that helped you get out of bed six hours later to change her diaper, and spend the next hour and forty-five minutes holding her and pacing as you tried to get her to sleep, when all she wanted to do was play with your nose. And again, it was the lower back that permitted you to spring from your chair during a staff meeting the next morning when your boss yelled, "Hey, Kremski, is that you snoring?"

These muscles were also essential when you tried to secure your squirming thirty-pound angel into her car seat while she played with the dog. And they were even more important several hours later when you had to gently remove her from her car seat while she was asleep. And it was the lower back muscles that made your mouth muscles whisper, "How come this child weighs 30 pounds awake and 345 pounds asleep?"

And years later, as your children got older and greedier, it was your lower back muscles that helped you perfect the *Pocket Pivot*, a maneuver you used every time your children's hands moved anywhere near your wallet.

(Note: Once you become a grandfather, you will no longer need the Pocket Pivot. When your grandchild looks up at you with those amazingly beautiful eyes and says, "Grandpa, can I please have a dollar?" you will not give it to her. Instead, you will give her your wallet, your credit cards, your PIN, and any municipal bonds you have on hand.)

But now, with your children gone from home, you have tried to limit the non-recreational use of your lower back muscles to less strenuous duties like putting on your socks and picking up the remote control.

However, sometimes your wife will have other plans for these muscles—plans that involve unloading things like bags of groceries or sacks of potting soil from the trunk of her car. Hopefully, you've invested wisely enough to be able to have your groceries delivered and hire a gardener.

But when you have grandchildren, all of these muscles will be tested once again. When this happens, it is helpful to draw on what is known as *muscle memory*, a physiological phenomenon whereby muscles are able to remember and echo repeated actions. Unfortunately, by the time most of us become grandfathers, the only *muscle memory* we have is the memory of once having muscles. Because if we still had *true* muscle memory, how would we explain going out to our local golf course and shooting 92 one day and 148 the next?

But do not despair. I have unearthed a few devices to help you tone your muscles and get into "grandfather shape." Although I have used neither of these methods, both come highly recommended from some of my more creative grandfather friends. These exercises can be done in the comfort of your own home, thus protecting you from any urge to join a fitness center, where you would have to grunt, sweat, and try to hold in your stomach in front of all those young ladies who don't need to be at the gym in the first place.

First, I know many grandparents who enjoy a nice quiet beverage together at the end of their day. Whether you drink water or something stronger, this custom gives you an opportunity to relax after another busy day of playing dominoes or clipping coupons. For those of you who'd like to multi-task during your cocktail hour, you only need to go to your local sporting goods store and purchase a small, weighted wrist belt. However, you need not put this on your wrist, as these contraptions have been known to cause perspiration and, in some cases, a nasty little rash. Rather, you should attach the weighted belt to the bottom of your glass. However, if you are drinking a cocktail and you've chosen to load it down with an olive, onion, or cherry, be sure to reduce the weight in the belt accordingly. You don't want to overdo it. And no matter what your beverage of choice is, it's important that you sip slowly, thus performing enough reps to maximize the muscle restoration process.

The second option takes a little more work and is best suited to homes with high ceilings. First, have your local handyman build a three-foot-high platform in your kitchen, with a ramp leading to the summit. Second, recruit two neighborhood teenagers strong enough to bench press Rush Limbaugh, and ask them to place your refrigerator atop the platform. Voila! With the ramp at a fifteen-degree incline, you have created a wonderful apparatus that will build up your calves and thighs every time you sneak off for a snack.

This type of device will also serve you well in your bathroom, with your toilet bowl atop the platform. If you get up in the middle of the night as often as I do, it will work wonders for your cardiovascular system.

But for those of you who aren't exercise fanatics, there are some preventative steps you can take to lessen the muscle demands required of grandfatherhood.

Because you'll be belting your grandchild into a modern car seat, many of which are the size and weight of a lunar landing module, you may want to reconsider buying that hot, sexy little two-door convertible you and your wife have been eyeing to celebrate your last child finding his own address. Dealing with an infant's car seat in such a confined area will very likely put you in traction, so you might need a slightly larger vehicle.

With a wide-body Winnebago, you'll have plenty of room to secure your resistant grandchild into his safety seat without rupturing any vertebrae—his or yours. You'll also have plenty of extra room to tote all the high-tech equipment and gadgets that today's babies seem to require: Strollers that convert into one-room condos with Murphy beds, high chairs that fold into Volvos, and potty seats that come with headphones and plasma screens.

It's also a good idea to have several excuses handy that will explain why grandpas don't do certain recreational activities.

"Buh-Buh, get down on your hands and knees so we can play pony ride," pleaded my four-year-old granddaughter Alexandra.

"I'd like to, sweetheart," I said to her. "But I can't. I hurt my back in the war."

"You were in a war?" she asked, impressed. "Which one?"

"Yes, Buh-Buh," my wife said with a smug smile. "Which war was that again?" This was patently unfair, because Jill knew full well that during the height of the Vietnam "conflict" I somehow managed to spend my entire four-year enlistment at an Air Force base in western Massachusetts. That may sound cushy to some, but if you check your history books, you'll find that because of me, the strategic communities of Holyoke and Chicopee Falls remain free to this day. Jill also knows that my entire Air Force stint was spent as a clerk-typist. Our squadron motto was "We don't retreat! We backspace!"

I've learned that in situations like this, wives do not go out of their way to be overly helpful. That's because they're grand*ma*s and not grand*pa*s; and grand*ma*s are very rarely asked by their grandchildren to do things like wrestle or play pony ride. They may be asked to help the child draw a pony, or even to make cookies that are shaped like ponies; but sciatica-inducing pony rides seem to be grandpa territory.

Or so my wife thought until I turned the tables on her.

"Maybe Grandma would like to play pony ride with you," I suggested to Alexandra. "She wasn't in a war."

Alexandra looked up at Jill. "Can *you* give me a pony ride, Grandma?"

Jill stared at me. It's the look she uses whenever I outwit her. I remembered seeing it only once before, about twenty years ago.

"I can't," she told Alexandra. "I hurt my back, too."

"How?" the girl demanded.

"How?" Jill answered, noticing that I was waiting for her answer as well. "Well, I hurt it when I had to carry around your poor old grandfather after his war injury."

Alexandra's eyes lit up with admiration. And then the two of them headed off to the kitchen to make cookies that looked like ponies.

"Welcome to
another EXCITING
Antiques
Roadshow!"

EIGHT

COMMUNICATION ARTS

Social scientists have suggested that couples who have been together for many years sometimes take on some of their partners' traits. These scientists further suggest that in some cases, couples of grandparent age may actually begin to look like each other. I hope and pray that this is not in store for my wife, who is considered by all to be a beautiful and refined woman. But I'm sure this assessment would change should she start becoming more like me, sprouting neck hair and scratching herself in public.

Another thing that changes with long-time couples is the way they communicate. I've observed that as we get older, my wife and I seem to have less to say to each other. This is not because we love each other less or care about each other less. Quite the opposite. It is because, as grandparents, we usually have fewer things to talk about than we did when we were younger. Things like our young children, our jobs, or disco. And because we spend most of our waking hours together, it follows that—should something exciting should happen in your life—like your SecureHorizons health plan announcing that it will begin covering tummy tucks, it's likely to happen to the both of you, which means there's not much to talk about, because you were both there in the first place.

Because you spend so much time together, it's highly unlikely that while you and your wife are watching a special on the Spanish Inquisition that you will turn to her and say, "Darn, honey, I almost forgot. Did I tell you that, while you were volunteering at the hospital yesterday, I had lunch with Antonio Banderas? He ordered the paella."

As further evidence that older couples talk less, I want you to recall the last time you and your wife were in a restaurant, and a younger couple sitting nearby had to call over to your table, "Hey, you two think you could pipe down a little?"

There's another reason people who have been together a long time speak to each other less. We've developed our own personal shorthand. We need fewer words to get our message across.

Think back to a cold winter night twenty-five years or so ago. It's nearly 11:30, and your children are all fast asleep; and when you snuggle up to your wife, there's a lot more than dreams of sugarplums dancing though your head. You gently put your arms around her and kiss her neck, complimenting her on her perfume. You even say how lovely she looks in that full-length flannel nightgown. When she hears that, she knows where you're headed.

"Sweetie, I'd love to, but I am absolutely exhausted, plus it's my morning to drive carpool tomorrow, so I have to get up even earlier to make the kids' lunches. Night, honey. I love you."

Then she kisses you, clicks the remote, and hands it to you. As she rolls over for her short trip to slumberland, at least you hear a comforting voice:

"And now … Heeeeeeerrre's Johnny!"

But now that you're of grandfather age, the same situation might very well go like this:

"Honey?" you say sweetly.

"Get real," she says.

So you grab the remote and switch on *Antiques Roadshow.* Shorthand.

But you will learn that when a grandchild enters your life, much of your shorthand will disappear faster than free meatballs at Bingo Night.

Here's how it goes where I live…

Because it's just the two of us at home, when I hear car keys jingling, I react like Pavlov's dog. I know it means that Jill is about to leave the house.

"Where are you off to?" I ask, already knowing her answer.

"Out," is all she ever chooses to tell me. And these days, it seems she very rarely requests the pleasure of my company.

And I am fine with this, because the places wives go when they go *out* are not usually places husbands want to go.

And though I don't know exactly where *out* is, I do know that when Jill does go *out*, it often involves spending a fair amount of money on things like the new microwave she recently bought. I also know where Jill's out *isn't*. Experience has taught me that *out* isn't anywhere near the do-it-yourself-doggie wash, the self service car wash, or any other place that would require Jill to do something that she has determined I should do.

We both think this is a fine arrangement.

But not long ago, a brush salesman knocked on my door.

"Hello," said the thirty-year-old man wearing a cheap tie and a white shirt with a collar two sizes larger than his neck. "Is your wife home?"

"No, she's out," I said, wanting to get back to the kitchen and the new microwave. When he knocked, I had just started nuking a pepperoni pizza, which is an illegal substance when Jill is home, as she claims the smell makes her nauseous. But since Jill's nose went out with her, it will not be offended.

"When will she be home?" the brush salesman asked.

"I don't know," I responded impatiently.

"You don't know?" This young man apparently found it inconceivable that a husband wouldn't know where his wife was, or when she was coming home. He probably suspected Jill was holed up inside, hiding from him behind the sofa. "Where did she go?" he asked, looking in suspiciously.

"Out," I told him.

"Out where?"

"I dunno. *Out* out." My voice rose slightly because the microwave beeped, letting me know that my frozen pizza would be ready as soon as I added my customary three pounds of Parmesan.

"Are you telling me that your wife went out and you don't know where she is?" he asked, appalled at meeting such a dunderheaded, negligent husband. I could tell this was no longer simply about brushes.

I noticed a wedding ring on his finger. "How long have you been married?" I asked.

"Two years," he said proudly.

I chuckled. "I suppose you know exactly where your wife goes when she goes out."

"Yes, I do," he said, doing his best to make me feel ashamed.

"Good," I said. "Then go wherever that is, and my wife is probably nearby. Have a nice day."

But when our grandchild is visiting and I hear the keys jingling in the other room, I don't even have to ask where Jill is going, because I will soon know the complete itinerary.

"Oh, you look so sweet!" I hear her say to Claire, our six-month-old granddaughter. Keep in mind that Claire barely understands two words: "bottle" and "more." But that doesn't stop Jill from throwing our shorthand right out the window and suddenly becoming an AARP tour guide.

"We are going to have such fun today!" Jill says to Claire, depositing her into her $20,000, 8-cylinder stroller. "And we have sooo much to do! First, we have to go to the market and pick up things for dinner. Then, we'll stop at the bakery on Elm and buy a pie for dessert. It's right next door to the dry cleaners, so we'll stop there and pick up Buh-Buh's shirt that he spilled pasta sauce all over." Claire chuckled at that. It seems my eating mishaps bring joy to everyone's life.

"Then we'll go to Baby World," Jill continued, "so we can get you a new outfit before we have your six-month picture taken at the mall! On our way home, we'll go visit my friend Mady so she can see what a beautiful little girl you are, okay?"

Then something even more unexpected came out of Jill's mouth: "Want to go with us, Buh-Buh?"

"What?" I thought. "Me? She asked me to go *out*?" I briefly considered it, but then I remembered that I had plans for when Jill was out. Big plans.

I was about to beg off when I saw Claire smiling up at me with a smile that said, "C'mon, go with us. You can hold me while Gaji shops, and I promise I won't spit up in your shirt pocket like I did in church."

"I'll be ready in five minutes," I said. As I hurried upstairs, I noticed my stomach bouncing with each step I took. That was all the proof I needed to convince me that scrapping my original plan was definitely the right decision. That other frozen pepperoni pizza would be much better off without me.

Chee

NINE

THE VERDICT? NOT GUILTY!

As fun and as rewarding as grandchildren can be, and as much as I strive to be a perfect grandfather, there was one development I did not anticipate. When it happens to you—and happen it will—it will likely hit you like a brick. It's not pretty, but it's inevitable; and even the most dedicated and loving grandfather will have to deal with it.

"It" occurs most frequently after your grandchild has reached the age of four and has more energy than a twelve-pack of Red Bull. And "it" often coincides with the first time you take care of her for longer than a weekend without her parents lurking to make sure that you feed her properly, get her to bed on time, and promise to watch your language while she's around.

For those of you who haven't yet soloed with your post-toddler grandchild, you should know that this takes mounds of preparation. I hope my experience will be helpful.

The first thing we did was to contact everyone we know (some of whom we haven't spoken to since the Eisenhower administration) to casually let them know—should they get the urge to call us to get together—that we were not available the following week.

"We'll be too wonderfully busy tending to our beautiful grandchild," we told them. "What? You didn't know we had a grandchild? Oh, I know we look way too young for that, but it's true. If you don't believe us, go to our website, www.coolestgrandparentsonthisoranyotherplanet.org."

The next thing we did was check with the child's mother to find out what supplies and provisions we'd need for the week. In addition to items like No More Tears shampoo and Mr. Bubble bath foam, she said that our granddaughter liked frozen waffles, bologna, white bread, mayonnaise, creamy peanut butter, pizza in a pocket, and several different brands of sugared cereal.

And finally, she said firmly, "But no junk food."

After renting a U-Haul to get the groceries home, I decided to make up another list: things to do with our granddaughter for the five days she'd be with us. I wanted the week to be perfect, so I settled on the beach, Disneyland, the San Diego Zoo, and a G-rated movie.

I figured that should be enough for Day One.

When Friday afternoon rolled around, I'd done everything on my list—and then some—to make sure everything was perfect for our little angel's arrival. I even spent two hours studying our television's instruction manual so I could program the remote to automatically locate Nickelodeon and the Disney Channel. But when I still couldn't figure it out, Jill asked the nine-year-old from next door come over. It took her less then three minutes.

When she saw my expression of inadequacy, the little girl did her best to make me feel better.

"It's okay, Mr. M.," she said. "My grandpa doesn't know how to do this either. And he's younger than you."

"Oh? How old is he?"

"Eighty-three, I think. Bye!"

By Friday evening, the two of us were so excited that we peeked through the front drapes every time we heard a car approaching. Where are they? They said they'd drop her off at 5:30, and it's already 5:35. How irresponsible and inconsiderate of them! When they finally did pull into our driveway, we tackled each other trying to be the first out the door to get to our granddaughter.

As we unloaded her things from the car, our son-in-law said he'd like to use the bathroom. When he tried to get out of the car, I pushed him back in and told him he'd have to wait; there was a very clean restroom at a nearby gas station.

Have a nice weekend, kids! Bye-bye!

And as they drove off in an SUV the size of our first apartment, we held our granddaughter's hand and hoped that maybe they'd decide to extend their five-day getaway to six … or maybe even seven.

But they stuck to their schedule. In fact, they returned an hour early. And when they put our granddaughter into her car seat, she told them that she had "the most funnest weekend ever!"

That made us feel very good.

And as they drove away, we stood and waved good-bye. As Jill continued waving her hand like a beauty queen in a parade, I glanced at her, expecting to see a tear or two. But instead, I saw a pair of eyes that looked exactly like Wile E. Coyote's after he's been steamrolled by the Road Runner. I suspected that I had that look, too, but I was too exhausted to lift a mirror to check.

Once their car was out of sight, we turned to each other and immediately realized that we both shared the same terrible thought. But how could that be? We love our granddaughter more than life itself.

Then why were we so happy to see her go?

What kind of grandparents are we?

An hour after they left, we were still beating ourselves up for feeling so good that our little angel was back where she belonged. Finally, we decided that if we were going to continue to chew on our own guilt, it might taste better combined with some Chinese food.

And it was while we were in the restaurant waiting for our "to go" order that we first saw her: the mysterious woman we still refer to as "Our Lady of Fung Lum's."

She was a bit older and was standing by herself as she perused the menu; I could tell she was having a tough time deciding what to order.

Finally, she approached Jill. "Excuse me, dear," she asked in an Irish accent thicker than a pint of warm Guinness, "but have you had the orange chicken here before?"

"I have," I said. "It's terrific."

"Thank you. I think my husband will enjoy that. He was going to come with," she said. "But he couldn't get out of his chair."

"Bad back?" I asked.

"No, exhaustion," she said with a laugh. "We had our grandchildren this weekend and they just left. Jesus, Mary, Joseph … peace and quiet at last."

Hearing this, we sensed that here was someone who would understand our pain. After she placed her order, we told her about our last five days. She listened patiently with an experienced smile.

"I'm sure your granddaughter is a beautiful girl," she said, sensing how we felt. "My four are absolute angels," she continued. "We love them dearly and would do anything for them. But that doesn't mean we want them around every minute, now does it?"

My wife and I exchanged relieved glances.

"It's like taking a vacation abroad," the lady continued. "Every sight you see is more wonderful than the last. You love every moment of your trip. But after a while, you start missing your own home. But that doesn't mean you didn't like your trip, now does it? No. It's just time for your bonnet to be hanging on your own hat rack."

Jill looked at me and smiled. Her Wile E. Coyote eyes were gone.

"Our grandchildren stay with us often, and we always enjoy it when they do," the lady said. "But every time their parents come to pick them up, I think of a little poem I heard years ago."

And then she recited in her delightful brogue:

I've seen the lights of Paris.
I've seen the lights of Rome.
But the most beautiful lights I've ever seen
Are the taillights of the grandchildren going home.

As we laughed at this, we were told that our order was ready. We paid the bill and started out, feeling 1,000% better than when we walked in.

"It was wonderful talking to you," we said to our new Irish friend as we opened the door to leave.

"Likewise. And I hope you enjoy a nice, quiet dinner," she said.

Same to you, Our Lady of Fung Lum's.

Same to you.

"Get-Tee-Oh!!!"

TEN

SPARE THE ROD . . .

I've learned that the difference between how I disciplined my own children versus how I discipline my grandchildren is not unlike the difference between taking a shower by myself or taking one with my Great Aunt Flossie. The first occurs daily, but the other will only happen if the future of mankind depends on it. And with global warming, super-sizing, and cheese sauces, how much time do I really have anyway?

I recall that I rarely disciplined my own children before they reached the age of eighteen months—unless they did something seriously wrong—like hit one of their siblings with a croquet mallet, used the contents of their diapers for finger paints, or made fun of my haircut.

Disciplining begins around this age because this is normally when a child begins to learn the concept of right and wrong. Not coincidentally, it is also just after he has learned that by standing up and walking like you do, he can get from *Point A* to *Point B* faster than he can on his knees. And often, he can also get there a lot faster than you can, which is why most trouble is located at *Point B*. Because if a child could break something valuable at *Point A*, there'd be no reason to go to *Point B* in the first place.

Your advantage as a grandfather is that you've learned this and a lot more during your years as a father. But your grandchild's parents have yet to learn it, and probably don't know that you already know it, because they still believe that their parents don't know much of anything. And it won't be until your grandchild is about eleven—and causing them to consider auctioning him off on eBay—that they'll realize how much you do know, *and* that you've known it all along.

And all that learning comes from your experience as a father. There is nothing more important for a grandfather than experience, except perhaps having a prostate smaller than an overripe mango. And one of the many things experience has taught you is that while it's very difficult to discipline your *child* before she's eighteen months old, it's even more difficult to discipline your *grandchild* before she's, say, forty-five.

And why is this? Because we want our grandchildren to like us. Back when you were a parent, you didn't expect your children to like you. In fact, they weren't *supposed* to like you, unless they also liked going to bed earlier than they thought they should, studying as much as you insisted, and having you drop them off at school and giving them a big good-bye kiss in front of their friends.

The only parents who worried about their children liking them were the zany few who claimed, "I want to be my child's best friend." Do you know who I wanted to be my children's best friend? The straight-A student who lived three doors down, with a school teacher mother and a Marine drill sergeant father. What's more, this family also had a dog trained to sniff out a) illegal substances and b) socks that have been worn to school more than six days in a row.

So whether our children liked us or not, they were stuck with us. We hoped that if we loved them and nurtured them while they were growing up, maybe they'd find time to like us later on.

But because we so desperately want our grandchildren to think we're the greatest thing since SpongeBob SquarePants, we have trouble disciplining them.

I don't know any grandmother who has ever threatened a grandchild with, "You just wait till your grandfather gets home!" There are a couple of simple reasons for this. First, grandfathers are usually home to begin with; and second, a grandmother knows that rather than disciplining his granddaughter, a grandfather will instead say that *all* children misbehave sometimes, then give his beautiful four-year-old granddaughter a crisp five-dollar bill.

Let's look at two common scenarios where virtually everything is the same except for one thing. In the first, think back to when you were a young dad. It's 12:30, Friday night, and you and your wife of six years come home after a rare night out with friends. Your babysitter tells you that your one-and-a-half-year-old was a perfect angel.

"She went to sleep without any complaining at all," she tells you. Then she adds, "Your baby is definitely the sweetest and smartest child I have ever been around in my whole life."

You're thrilled with this assessment, even though your sitter is only fifteen, and hasn't been around many children because a) she is an only child, and b) she is home schooled. (A few years later, you'll learn that she left home—and therefore, school—to pursue her lifelong dream of becoming a magician's assistant.)

After driving your sitter home, you and your wife get to bed around one. When she yawns, you try to win some romantic points by hugging her and volunteering to get up with the baby in the morning so she can sleep in. And though she is thankful, your only reward is a tender good-night kiss and instructions to make sure your daughter eats all her cereal for breakfast.

The next morning, you hear your daughter stirring in her room at 6:30. At 6:31, you go back to sleep. At 6:42, you hear her whimpering. At 6:43, you go back to sleep. At 6:45, your wife elbows you … hard. At 6:45:05, you decide it would be a good time to get up with the baby.

After changing your daughter's diaper with your eyes half open, you stumble into the kitchen and deposit her in her high chair. Then you go to the refrigerator and grab breakfast for both of you: cereal and milk for her; a slice of three-day old sausage pizza and a half-empty quart bottle of soda for you. You set her cereal and milk on her tray, and just in case your enormously gifted child is unsure about what to do with the cereal, you rub your tummy and say "Mmm, mmm."

She looks at you curiously, then says, "Naaahhh." And as you slug down the flat Mountain Dew, she pushes the cereal off her tray and onto the floor.

You can't believe it. Your little angel has never done anything like that before! What did that maverick home-schooler teach her?

So while your dog thinks he's hit the jackpot and happily laps up the spillage, you go and get another bowl. When you open the pantry for more cereal, your daughter spots something in there.

"Geh-tee-oh," she yells, pointing to a can of SpaghettiO's.

Although you think that's very cute, you also know your duties as a father.

"Honey, SpaghettiO's are not for breakfast."

"Geh-tee-oh!" she insists.

"No, sweetie, you have cereal for breakfast," you tell her as you place another full bowl in front of her.

"No! Geh-tee-oh," she yells. And then she pushes the second bowl onto the floor.

You stare at your daughter. She looks at you defiantly, and then gives you that strained, red-faced look that indicates that her defiance has taken the form of her soiling her just-changed diaper.

"Geh-tee-oh!"

So there you are: Two gunfighters in the old West. High noon, Main Street.

But you're the sheriff of this town. You know what you have to do, even though you hate to do it.

"Throwing cereal is a bad girl," you tell her, trying to sound stern. Then you take her tiny hand in yours and give your hand a firm smack, a move fathers know is like throwing marshmallows at a man in full body armor.

She looks at you, stunned at the sound, and her eyes become as big as Frisbees. She wants to cry, but she can't, because her lungs won't allow her to let out any air while she curls her quivering lower lip. (This is a move that she'll learn to perfect as she gets older, and will usually employ when the discussion involves boyfriends, curfews, or how that dent got in your car.) When she's finally able to exhale, it's a good one. That's because all of that retained air produces a scream that would make Howard Dean proud. Glasses shatter. Dogs run for cover. Except your dog, who's happily slurping up his second bowl of milk and cereal and trying to remember why he was so jealous when you first brought this little creature home.

"Waaaaaaaahhhhh!"

And although you know you did the right thing, you feel terrible about it. You remove your wailing daughter from her high chair and hold her.

"There, there. It's okay, honey. Daddy didn't mean it."

"Waaaaaaaahhhhh!"

"What did you do?!" demands a sleepy, unhappy voice.

You turn to see your wife glaring at you. The dog also sees her and cowers under the table. Sometimes it's good to be a dog.

"Well..." you start to explain.

"It's all right, sweetie," she says to the baby as she takes her from you. Then she takes a whiff of your daughter's diaper. "Doesn't Daddy know how to change a diaper?"

You start to explain, but before you can get a word out, your wife says to the baby, "Don't worry, honey. Mommy's here now."

Then she and your daughter disappear, leaving you alone with the dog, who determines that it's safe to return to his milk and cereal.

You sit and worry that your beautiful daughter will hate you forever. But a few hours later when you're sadly watching your alma mater's football team get pummeled, your cereal-tossing daughter toddles in, just when the other team scores another touchdown, making it 1,770 to 3.

"Oh no," you say. "This is horrible."

"That's okay, Daddy," she says, climbing onto your lap. "*I* love you."

Then she gives you a big kiss.

And the world is a wonderful place to be.

Now, I want you to look at the same scenario twenty-five years later. You are now the *grandfather* of an eighteen-month-old.

Once again it's Friday night. But instead of a late night out with friends, you and your wife are at home yawning and playing Scrabble. It's 9:30. The game has taken a little longer than normal because the outcome will determine who gets up with your granddaughter in the morning. It's your final turn, as you hold the two remaining letters. Your wife has a twenty-point lead and smiles at you victoriously. But just as you're ready to concede defeat, you see it: a place for your *Q-U*! You put it in front of the word "ILL" and you win!

You spring to your feet, do some nifty dance moves, and cheer. You see the defeat in your wife's eyes.

"Oh, pipe down," she says. "You'll wake your granddaughter."

You glide over and kiss her. "It's okay, sweetie, maybe next time," you gloat. "But tomorrow? *I* get to get up with her!"

The next morning, you and your granddaughter are enjoying breakfast together. She is on her second helping as you force your way through your bowl of cholesterol-lowering oatmeal and skim milk.

You hear your wife approaching. "Mornin', darling," you call.

"Good morning, love," she says. Then she looks at her granddaughter in her high chair.

"My goodness!" she asks. "What is that all over her?"

You look at your perfectly happy granddaughter, whose angelic face is covered with tomato sauce and noodles.

"SpaghettiO's," you tell her.

"SpaghettiO's? For breakfast? Where did she get an idea like that?"

"It's what she wanted," you tell her.

"Oh," says your wife. "Well, then, give me a bowl, too."

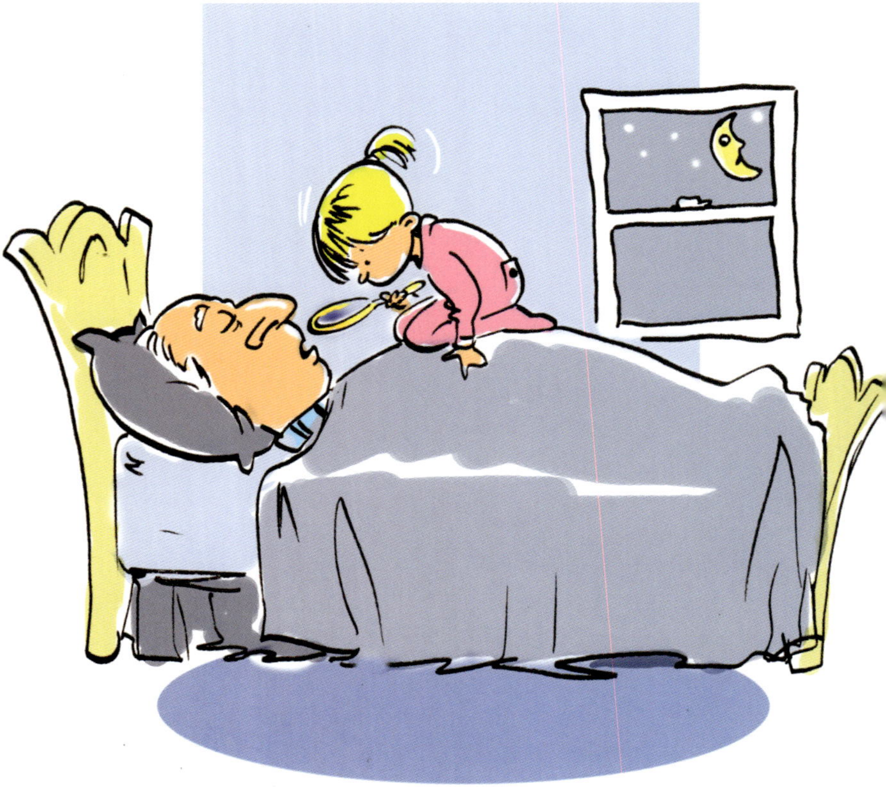

ELEVEN

WHEN THE LITTLE HAND IS ON THE SEVEN

Like most grandfathers whose children have been out of the house for a while, and who have shown no desire to return for any period longer than a Sunday dinner, I have thoroughly "de-childrened" our home. This means that once again I can use the bathroom at any time without needing a reservation or a book of matches, I can now open a bottle of aspirin without requiring the Jaws of Life to remove the childproof cap, and I can spend an entire day at home without once hearing the word "dude."

I'm sure it didn't take you and your wife very long to get back into the routine of "just the two of you," which opened up a world that you had almost forgotten about, a world where weekends are yours again. Now you can start out with some nice Saturday morning lounging, some brisk Saturday afternoon exercise, and some soothing Saturday evening Aleve.

I have a friend who is a board-certified Emergency Room Physician. His real name is Michael, but everyone—co workers included, calls him "Zip." Now although this may be an endearing nickname, it is not one that I'd like to hear if I were brought into the ER because, say, I was hit by a car. "Don't worry, Mr. Milligan," the nurse says to me as I begin to lose consciousness. "You're lucky this happened tonight. Dr. Zip is here." I don't know about you, but I like my doctors to be named Arthur, Carl, or Edward.

Despite his nickname, Zip is an extremely intelligent and responsible man. Yet, within a week after his children moved out of the house, he called me and proclaimed, "This is great! We can do anything, even run around the house in our underwear if we want!"

I'd heard men use that expression before, but had never really given it any thought. But now, I suddenly had mental pictures—and not pretty ones—of my doctor friend running around his house in his skivvies. Thankfully, I have never seen Zip cavorting in his underpants and unless hell is even worse than it's cracked up to be, I never will. But just the thought of him in his living room, pirouetting around tables and somersaulting over sofas in his Fruit of the Looms is evidence enough that grandfathers having the freedom to run around in their underwear is not a good thing. And that it should not be guaranteed by the Constitution.

I am not ashamed to say that I don't like to *run* anywhere, unless it's really extremely urgent, like if I pull into the Denny's parking lot at 4:59, knowing the Senior Dinner Discount stops at 5:00. Also, I've recently discovered that when I run anywhere at my age, my belly button arrives at my destination about three minutes before I do. But even if I did enjoy a good run now and then, I would surely not do it in my underwear. And while I would certainly welcome the opportunity to watch my beautiful wife run around our house in *her* underwear, I think that's about as likely to happen as Britney Spears opening a chain of driving schools.

But whether you like to run around the house in your U-Trou, or just sit and enjoy the quiet, you will have to make some adjustments to your tranquil lifestyle now that you have grandchildren. One of the first changes you'll have to make is to your alarm clock.

You won't be needing it.

When we were younger and had jobs that required us to be at work on time, we often chose to ignore the alarm clock. That is why many of us often showed up for work with hair like Donald Trump's and breath like Donald Duck's.

But now that we're older—and in many cases, don't have to be anywhere at any particular hour—we set our alarms for earlier, which means we have much more time to do much less. This explains why so many men of grandfather age take up time-filling hobbies like gardening, golf, and eating dinner at 2:30 in the afternoon.

But you will learn that no matter what time you wake up in the morning, your grandchild will be awake at least a half-hour earlier.

And although a grandchild will tiptoe into your room while you're sleeping, she will not immediately wake you. That is because before her parents dropped her off for their romantic weekend getaway, they told her, "Grandma and Grandpa are old. Let them sleep until they wake up. And if they don't wake up by 9:30, hold a mirror under their noses like I showed you. Then call 911."

And while your granddaughter won't wake you, what she *will* do is hold her breath and put her face about one millimeter from yours while you sleep. But soon, unless she has the lungs of a Japanese pearl diver, she will begin breathing as she waits for you to open your eyes.

It won't be long before you become aware that someone is very close to you, and that her unique breath has the unmistakable aroma of a youngster who hasn't yet learned the value of a toothbrush. It's now that you have a critical decision to make. You can keep your eyes closed and pretend you're still in a deep slumber, hoping this will buy you a few more minutes of sleep while she loses interest. You should know, however, that most grandchildren can wait out Rip Van Winkle.

Or you may try to peek, opening your eyes a micrometer, thinking your grandchild will not notice. But before you attempt this, be warned that grandchildren have the eyes of a hawk, and that a hawk can see a gopher blink from 1,000 feet. So unless you've always wanted to be an airsick gopher, keep your eyes closed.

Probably the best course of action is for you to open your eyes as wide as you can and pretend you've been awake for an hour. Then say to your granddaughter, "Good morning, beautiful. How did you sleep?!"

"Good," she says. "Can we play Uncle Wiggly now?"

As you try to remember what she's talking about, you recall that last night you played so many games of Uncle Wiggly that you never want to see his chubby cheeks or cutesy overalls again. In fact, because of your years of endlessly playing this simplistic board game with your own children, you have developed a serious dislike for Uncle Wiggly, and uncles in general.

Last night she had asked, "Just one more game, grandpa? Please?"

"You have to go to bed, honey," you said. (Note: This is grandfather-speak for, "*I* have to go to bed, honey.")

"Okay. But can we play Uncle Wiggly again in the morning?" she asked.

"Sure," you said.

"Promise?"

CAUTION: *The Surgeon Grandfather has determined that saying "Promise" to a grandchild can have serious consequences.*

You should use this word only if you mean it. Do not use it as freely as you did with your own children, when you could wiggle out of promises by re-promising.

"Daddy, can we go to JollyLand next Saturday?"

"Sure."

"Promise?"

"Promise."

Then when you got home from work on Friday night, you had to break the bad news. "Kids, we can't go to JollyLand tomorrow. I have to work."

"But you promised us!"

"Yes, I did. But long before I promised you that, I promised your mother that we would always live in a nice house. And that our house would have a roof and would not be attached to a pick-up truck."

"But Daddy..."

"We'll go next weekend. Promise."

"Okay, but we get to stay until it closes, okay?"

"Promise."

This ploy does not work with a grandchild, because a grandchild does not accept negotiation. Instead, if you break a promise, she will break off all discussion and look at you with a hurt and disappointment that you haven't seen since her hamster got out of his cage and you accidentally backed over it with your car.

But even then, you were able to save the day (but unfortunately, not the hamster) by telling her that little Herbie wasn't dead, just a little sick. And then you told her that when she went in for her nap, you would go to the pet store and get a secret hamster medicine that only smart grandpas know about. And when she wakes up, Herbie will be just fine.

"Promise?" she asked.

"Promise," you promised.

And sure enough, when she woke up from her nap and ran out to her hamster cage, there was Herbie, looking fit as a fiddle, although she did mention that he seemed a teensy bit chubbier.

"That's because the medicine makes him a little a little fatter," you explained.

"You mean like your medicine?" she asked.

Back at your bedside, your granddaughter continues, "C'mon, Grandpa let's play Uncle Wiggly. You promised."

"All right, honey," you say as you pull yourself out of bed. "But first I think someone needs to brush their teeth."

"You're right, Grandpa," she says, sensing an odor. "But hurry up. And don't wake Grandma."

TWELVE

GRANDCHILD PROOFING

In addition to your alarm clock, I can tell you with confidence that there are several other things in your house that you will not be using when your grandchildren visit. I am not suggesting that you need to hide these things from your grandchildren, but you may want to hide them from yourself so you aren't constantly reminded how much you miss them.

Bathroom Reading Material

If your grandchildren stay with you for an extended period of time, which means longer than, say, three hours and forty-five minutes, you will have to put your normal routine on hold until they are on their way home again. Although you know that your young grandchildren are beautiful, intelligent and all kinds of wonderful, you'll learn that there's another thing they are: *there*. And when they are *there*, it seems their favorite place to be is wherever you are.

It's no revelation that older men put a high value on proper bathroom time. It's as much a part of our lives as food, clothing, and talking back to the television set. But finding quiet time when your grandchildren visit is very difficult, if not impossible. You have to learn to pick your spots, like when you see your wife and granddaughter

watching a video with a singing starfish. This is a good time to make your move because your wife is nodding off and your granddaughter is transfixed to the screen, even though she's been watching this video almost non-stop since she arrived. So you make your exit, newspaper folded under your arm.

You enter the bathroom and shut the door very quietly.

As you get ready to catch up on what's been going on in the world since your grandchild arrived, you listen very closely. The only sound you hear is your wife and granddaughter singing in the distance, "*I'm Sam the Starfish, that's who I am. I live in the ocean with Calvin the Clam!*"

But as you sit and unfold the newspaper, don't think you're in the clear. Soon, you hear the doorknob turn. But it won't open, since one of the things you learned from years of being a father is to always lock the bathroom door. And to store your wallet on a high dresser where no little people could reach it.

"Grandpa, are you in there?" your granddaughter calls through the door.

You know that your best bet is to remain silent.

"Yes, honey, I'm in here."

"Can I come in?"

"No, darling, you can't."

"Why?"

"Uh, just because. But I'll be out soon," you lie.

"What are you doing?" she asks.

You know that she knows exactly what you are doing. She has a bathroom at home. She knows what she does in there, and what her parents do in there. But, like lawyers, grandchildren enjoy asking questions they already know the answers to.

That's why they ask things like, "Isn't Grandma pretty?" "Do you want a back rub?" "Can I have a kiss?"

You decide that since she already knows what you're doing in the bathroom, there's no reason to be anything less than honest.

"What am I doing? I'm re-grouting the tile."

She has no idea what that means. So of course she says, "Really? Can I help?"

"I don't think so, honey. It's a very dangerous job," you tell her.

"That's okay, grandpa. I'm not afraid."

"I know you're not afraid. But are you certified?"

"What's that?"

"Certified. It means do you have enough education to re-grout tile?"

She thinks for a moment, then says, "I know my colors."

"What about math? What's two plus seven?"

There's a worried pause, then, "A million?"

"Well, I guess you *are* qualified. Yes, you can help. We'll start tomorrow."

"Promise?"

Careful now, Grandpa.

Your Golf Clubs

When your grandchildren are visiting for the weekend, you will not have time to play golf. You probably won't have time to watch golf, either. In fact, you'll be lucky to find time to even spell "golf."

If you don't believe me, just try running it by your wife.

"Honey, I know the grandkids are coming tomorrow, but rather than spending the entire day with all of you, I thought I'd take a little break—only five or six hours—to play some golf with Ernie and the guys while you and the four grandchildren go to the zoo, then grocery shopping. What do you say?"

When you regain consciousness and the attending physician asks you how your four iron found its way to that particular part of your body, my advice to you is to plead ignorance.

The Rules to Any Board or Card Game

Grandchildren want to win in everything they do. And no matter how hard you try to make sure that happens, following the rules can often get in the way. So unless you want them to like their other grandpa—the one with all the money and the winter home in Aspen—more than they like you, roll with it.

Any Deck with All 52 Cards

See above.

Ambien or Any Sleep Aid

Unless you live in a jet engine testing facility, when your grandchildren visit you will need absolutely nothing to help you get to sleep at bedtime. And to grandfathers, "bedtime" means any time after *Oprah*. Not only will you not need to take a pill, at the end of the day you will not have enough strength to open the bottle or to lift a glass of water to your mouth.

DRIVE-THRU
PHARMACY

THIRTEEN

"NOT TONIGHT, GRANDPA"

When I recall my own grandparents, many wonderful and lasting images and memories pop into my head: holiday dinners, old-smelling furniture, and stories about how they were so poor during the Great Depression that, even on the sunniest day, their family of seventeen could only afford one shadow. But when I think of my grandparents, there's one thing I have never thought about: sex.

And if any of *you* think of your grandparents in this way, you need to put down this book immediately and contact a licensed therapist.

It was difficult enough accepting that our *parents* were not always sleeping when they were in their bedroom. But our grandparents? Grandparents didn't have sex.

Well, today they do.

Or so I'm told.

And one of the reasons that grandmothers and grandfathers are smiling more these days? Viagra. This and similar medications have helped more grandfathers get back in the saddle than a Sun City riding instructor. Yet no one I talked to would admit that he ever once needed the assistance of these supplements, so I can only assume that either the sales figures for these products have been enormously inflated, or that my family, friends, and colleagues are lying through their dentures while looking at life through blue-tinted glasses.

It seems that the average man is very uneasy discussing such a matter, probably because he thinks he's the only guy on earth who suffers from occasional power outages. But if that were the case, why would pharmaceutical companies spend so much money promoting their products?

And it should be no surprise that the manufacturers of these items spend a good deal of their advertising dollars on televised sporting events—particularly golf—which is watched overwhelmingly by middle-aged men.

After extensive research, I can tell you without qualification that you will never see a Viagra commercial air during *Dora the Explorer*, or a Levitra spot featuring a recently-satisfied, gorgeous older couple during an episode of *Pimp My Ride*.

So why golf? Probably because it's a sport in which older men can still participate and feel competitive with other older men. All one has to do is be able to sit in a cart without falling out more than twice a round, hit a ball that's not moving, remember where it went, get back in the cart, ride another fifteen feet, and hit it again. The game's most difficult aspect is being clever enough to avoid paying for drinks afterwards.

Arguably, one of the most talented and admired athletes in any sport is New York Yankees shortstop Derek Jeter. But I think it's a safe bet that, after watching a baseball game where he has made one spectacular play after another, very few grandfathers jump off the sofa and say to their wives, "Honey, let's go outside so you can you hit me some grounders. I want to work on my double play move."

Or after watching an NFL game, we're not likely to shout out, "I'll be back in an hour, sweetie. I'm going down to the high school to lay some big licks on a tackling dummy."

But golf is different. When Tiger Woods wins yet another tournament, practice ranges are immediately stacked three-deep with grandfather-aged men who should know better than to go out in public dressed like that.

Erectile dysfunction (ED) is not like most medical conditions, where you need a doctor to tell you you've got it. You already know you've got it, and not only that, you remember the exact moment when you first learned you'd got it.

Also, it is not an affliction that anyone else would be aware that you have, unless you told someone—which is about as likely to happen as Keith Richards becoming a spokesman for a line of skin care products.

For example, if you suddenly started growing a second nose from your forehead, it would be obvious something was wrong with you; anyone might be tempted to stop you on the street and say, "Sir, your upper nose is running and it's dripping unpleasant-looking goo into your eye. Perhaps you should talk to a doctor about that."

That would be easy; but talking to a doctor about ED is an entirely different and uncomfortable proposition. So I dealt with it the way most men would: I put it off as long as possible. But my wife and I were celebrating our wedding anniversary in a week, and we have this long-standing tradition. So to speak.

Obviously, handling this over the phone would be far less humiliating, so after a few false starts I finally worked up the courage to call my doctor's office.

"Good morning, Dr. Funderbin's office. Danielle speaking."

"Shoot," I thought to myself. "Danielle!" She's the perky twenty-five-year-old who greets me with an attractive smile each time I make an office visit. Over time, I've managed to delude myself into thinking that she's harboring a harmless crush on me. This makes her the last person I want to know about my "problem."

"How may I help you?" Danielle asked.

"Yes," I said, lowering my voice at least twelve octaves. "I'd like to speak with Dr. Funderbin."

"What is the call regarding?" she asked.

"It's about a prescription," I told her in a voice so low that I sounded like Weezy from *The Jeffersons*.

"Is it for a sore throat?" Danielle asked helpfully. "You sound like you have a cold."

"No, it's not a cold. Could I please just speak to Dr. Funderbin?"

"He's with patients all morning. But if you like, I could put you through to his personal voice mail."

"Fine."

"Okay, I'll connect you. Leave a message and Melanie, his nurse, will call you back by the end of the day."

"Whoa!" I said, my voice involuntarily returning to normal. "Melanie? Why will *she* be calling me back?"

I don't like Melanie very much. She is a big-boned woman who thinks I'm a sissy because I whimper whenever she takes blood, a task she performs with the gentle touch of a prison guard.

"Is this Mr. Milligan?" asked Danielle, recognizing my real voice.

"No!" I lied. "Listen, I really need to speak to the doctor."

"Is this an emergency, Mr. Milligan?" Danielle asked impatiently.

"I am *not* Mr. Milligan! And yes, it *is* a bit of an emergency."

"Then you should hang up and dial 911 right away."

Oh, isn't that a fine idea? I imagined a scene where paramedics pull up to my house, sirens blaring. Two chiseled, terminally handsome young EMTs jump out and hurriedly wheel a gurney to my front door. Our neighbors gather outside, speculating on what could have happened to me this time. They're certain it couldn't be my wife, because she never does anything stupid.

Bob, who lives a few doors down and who I suspect runs a gambling business out of his garage, has started a pool on what might be wrong with me, and whether or not I will survive it. The early favorite seems to be "Gardening Accident," because someone recently saw me buying a weed whacker.

I let the paramedics in, and they're surprised to find me calm and pain-free. When I sheepishly explain my problem, one of them says, "Jeez, the way you sounded on the phone, we thought you had an extra nose growing out of your forehead or something."

"Yeah," says the other. "Or a four iron wedged in your backside."

And when they pack up to leave, they say, "For things like this, sir, you should just call your doctor."

Gee, thanks, fellas. I never thought of that.

But eventually, I swallowed my pride, talked to Melanie the Mangler, and then to my doctor, who agreed to write me a prescription. The worst was behind me, until I realized I still had to take my hard won Rx to the pharmacy.

There have been many important pieces of legislation enacted to insure that women have equal employment opportunities in whatever field they choose. I am all for that, but do so many of these women have to choose to become pharmacists?

Like many men who have reached grandfather age, I've become one of millions of lucky folks who now have a plastic pill container with the day of the week stenciled on each compartment. It also means that I've been trading at my local pharmacy for years, and whenever I go in there, they are professional, courteous, and prompt.

They also call me by my first name.

So of course there's no way I could take such a sensitive prescription to them. What would they think? The cream I needed for that rash last year was bad enough. But this?

So I devised a brilliant plan that would allow me to have my prescription filled with no further damage to my self-esteem. You are welcome to use it, if you dare.

First, I located a twenty-four-hour, drive-through pharmacy on the other side of town. Then I called and learned that working the midnight to 8:00 a.m. shift would be a new pharmacist named John. This fit my needs perfectly; by midnight, all my friends would have been asleep for at least four hours. And, as a bonus, I would be dealing with a male pharmacist, which would eliminate a lot of the embarrassment from the situation. As simple as that, I'd have my prescription in time for our anniversary, and no one would ever know a thing.

I tiptoed out of the house at five minutes before midnight for the twenty-five-minute trip to the pharmacy; when I arrived there were three cars ahead of me in the drive-through lane.

John the pharmacist had a mirror by his window so he could see how many cars were waiting. When he eyed me, he reacted strangely, suddenly seeming edgy and nervous about something. I assumed he had probably hoped for a slower evening.

A few minutes later, I was next in line. I gave a relieved sigh, knowing that before long I would have my magic pills and my little problem would be solved. I put my head back, closed my eyes, and began making plans for our anniversary.

That's when I heard the sirens and screeching tires. Before I knew it, two uniformed police officers were leveling their service revolvers at me.

"Get out of the car, slowly," they shouted. "And we don't want to see anything in your hands!"

To show them I wasn't holding anything, I dropped my suddenly-sweaty prescription form on the seat, got out of my car and held up my hands, hoping to send them a message that they were dealing with a man who was extremely compliant, obedient, and petrified.

While one of the officers quickly patted me down, the other asked what I had tossed on the seat before I got out of the car.

"A prescription, sir," I replied. I added the "sir" even though this officer was young enough to be my child.

"A prescription?" he said with suspicion. "You expect me to believe that?"

"You can check for yourself, officer."

When he confirmed that it was indeed a prescription and his partner had determined that I was unarmed, they relaxed a bit, relatively certain that I was not a threat.

"Why are you out here getting a prescription at this hour, dressed like that?" the officer asked, pointing to my face.

It's then I realized why they were being so cautious with me. I was still wearing the ski mask I put on when I left home to ensure that no would recognize me.

I took off the mask and the officer who had patted me down turned me to face him.

"Coach Mike?" he asked, amazed.

But I didn't immediately recognize him.

"It's me … Steve Porter," he said with a big grin. "I was on your Little League team, remember? The White Sox?"

"Oh, yes, Steve, hi. How are you doing?" I said, recalling that Steve didn't have a whole lot of baseball talent. Back then, he couldn't catch a thing. To make up for that, he now catches old men out skulking for Viagra.

"This was the best coach I ever had," Steve told his partner, who returned my prescription form to me.

"Nice to meet you, sir," he said. "Sorry about the confusion. Go ahead and get your prescription. But lose the ski mask, okay?"

And then Steve pointed at the prescription and said, "Have a good time, Coach." He followed this with a rakish wink and thumbs up.

I nodded, thanked them for their understanding, and waved as they drove off.

When I finally got home with my hard-earned pills, I felt relatively confident that no one would ever be the wiser.

But three days later, when I was walking my dog, I happened past the Porters' house. Mr. Porter was outside, watering his lawn.

"Hi, Gus," I said.

"Oh, hey!" he called back. Then after a short pause, he added, "How's it going, Casanova?" And he laughed so hard he wet himself with his hose.

Serves him right.

So now that I had what I needed, I planned to use it judiciously.

But not when our grandchildren are visiting.

Or, as my wife says, should I so much as touch her with grandkids asleep in the next room, "Don't get any big ideas."

It makes me think of a book I gave my mother many years ago when our first child was born. I believe it was called *Grandmothers Are to Love*. Well, around my house, we have an updated version. It's called *Grandmothers Are to Love, Except by Grandfathers When the Grandchildren Are Around*.

FOURTEEN

THE EYE OF THE BEHOLDER

As a grandfather, I will tell anyone who will listen that I have the cutest, smartest, and most talented grandchildren ever. And those whom I can't reach personally will surely get the message from my numerous bumper stickers or the "World's Greatest Grandpa" T-shirt I get every Father's Day.

I'm sure that you feel the same way about your grandchildren; and although you know that they are all things beautiful and wonderful, there will be a few hard-to-please folks who won't be as enthusiastic about them as you are.

I've found that people like this are not discerning; they are not visionaries; they are not appreciative of childhood genius.

And they are not grandparents.

As hard as it might be for you to understand, people of this type also may not appreciate the unbelievably delightful and always-riveting stories you love to tell about your grandkids.

None of this is to suggest that any of us will stop boasting about our grandkids. But—like eating onions at lunch time—bragging should be done at your own risk. If not, you may find your friends walking away from you whenever you open your mouth.

Consider the case of Steve and Eve Reeve and Larry and Mary Carey. (I changed their names to protect both our

WORLD'S
GREATEST
GRANDPA

friendships and the $35 "Steve" still owes me from a poker game.) These four long-time friends made a date to visit a Monet exhibition at their local museum and have dinner afterward. In addition to their interest in art, Steve and Eve and Larry and Mary have almost everything in common, except for one small but significant thing: Larry and Mary have a three-year-old grandson, Jerry. Steve and Eve have no grandchildren, although they do have a grown daughter who has a live-in boyfriend, a tortoise, and two iguanas she calls her "kids."

When the foursome met in front of the museum and started up the granite steps, Larry and Mary couldn't resist telling Steve and Eve about the previous weekend, when little Jerry had stayed with them.

"He is sooo darling," Mary said.

"And very mature for his age," added Larry, as they entered the high-ceilinged foyer, "Little Jerry is almost completely potty trained! Oh, sure, he has a little accident every now and then, but never with poop-poop, only with pee-pee," he crowed. His words bounced off the elegant marble colonnades as though he were using a bullhorn.

Then Mary told Steve and Eve that "Little Jerry already knows all his colors!" as they entered the main exhibition hall.

"And not just the primaries," Larry continued. "Hues and earth tones, too."

As they approached Monet's *Rouen Cathedral in Full Sunlight*, Steve uttered, "Amazing."

Thinking that Steve's "amazing" was referring to little Jerry, Larry agreed wholeheartedly. "Yes, he *is* amazing. His pre-school teacher says most kids don't grasp all that until they're five."

"I was talking about Monet's perspective of the cathedral."

"Oh, yes, it's lovely," Mary said quickly without really studying it. "And speaking of cathedrals, we took Jerry to church with us Sunday morning. We gave him a dollar to put in the collection, but when the basket got to us, he looked inside and said, 'Look, more money!' and grabbed a handful of bills."

Larry continued with a chuckle. "And when the usher tried to take the money back from him, Jerry started screaming 'My money! My money!' It was so cute!"

Steve and Eve looked at each other and wondered who these people were and what did they do with the real Larry and Mary?

Then Eve tried to get everyone to focus on the reason they were there: Monet's timeless works of art.

"Oh, my gosh," Eve gasped, staring at the painting of the cathedral. "Look at his use of yellow."

"And *dode*," said Larry, smiling to Mary in some secret grandparent code.

"*Dode*? What the hell's *dode*?" asked Steve.

"That's how Jerry says *gold*," explained Mary. "We were going to correct him, but it's so darn precious..."

When they moved on to Monet's famous depictions of water lilies, Steve and Eve wondered if Precious Little Jerry would pronounce them *willies*, because that's what they were getting a case of.

Gazing at one of Monet's most famous works, *Water Lilies and Clouds*, they were all taken by its beauty. But Larry seemed particularly moved.

"You won't believe this," he said, staring at one of the world's great works by one of its great artists, "but little Jer painted something just like that last weekend."

"Who's Jer?" asked another man who was admiring the work.

"Our grandson," explained Mary to the perfect stranger she was now addressing like a lifelong friend. "He's only three, see?" she said, pulling out her billfold and producing pictures of her artistic grandson. "He did it with his paint set. Two-dollar watercolors."

The man nodded and hurried off, looking at Steve and Eve sympathetically.

"Really, guys," Larry persisted. "I mean, it's not *exactly* the same, but if you look at it at kind of an angle..."

Steve and Eve stared dumbfounded as their two normally intelligent friends twisted their bodies just shy of standing on their heads to look at a perfectly beautiful picture upside down.

As they all walked toward the restaurant after the exhibit, Larry and Mary continued telling what seemed to be a never-ending collection of Adorable Little Jerry stories. Mary suggested to Larry that maybe they should start checking into art schools for him. But when Larry heard this, he thought she may be getting just a little ahead of herself. "Sure, Jerry has obvious artistic talent," Larry agreed. "But he may be an even better athlete!"

Larry then told Steve how he was tossing a Nerf football with Jerry and "the little guy has the arm of Peyton Manning!" Larry wasn't sure if major college football programs actually recruited three-year-olds, but he felt it was certainly worth investigating.

When Mary received a call on her cellular, Steve seized the opportunity to take Eve aside to whisper that he'd had it with Larry and Mary. And especially with Jerry.

Steve continued that it would only get worse at the restaurant. Whatever dish they ordered, Larry and Mary would undoubtedly tell the waiter that Jerry could have prepared it better. Perhaps Jerry will be the first three-year-old college quarterback painter to attend Le Cordon Bleu! He could even design the menu covers!

Then Steve told Eve that they needed to come up with an excuse to get out of going to dinner.

Eve understood Steve's pain. She was tired of it, too. But Larry and Mary were good friends, and she wouldn't do anything to hurt their feelings. So she told Steve that he'd just have to cowboy up; there was absolutely no way she was going to be a part of any lame plan to get out of having dinner with Larry and Mary. Steve should be ashamed of himself for even considering such a thing, she told him.

When Mary concluded her phone call, she had exciting news for everyone. Of all the luck, little Jerry and his parents were in the neighborhood and they were going to join them for dinner! How great was that?

It's at this part of the story that that you should know that Eve and Steve have always considered themselves to be above-average athletes. Eve was a nationally ranked college gymnast and skier; she continues playing competitive adult soccer and volleyball, and regularly trains in Tae Bo and yoga.

Steve gets his exercise by playing in a weekly poker game.

Because of her athleticism, Eve was limber enough to break her fall when she tripped over the curb across the street from the restaurant.

When Larry and Steve saw her go down, they rushed to her assistance, helping her to her feet.

"You okay, Eve?" Larry asked as she tried to put weight on her foot.

"Agh! I don't think so," moaned Eve, grabbing her ankle. "I think I sprained it."

"We need to get some ice on that," said Steve with great concern.

"I'm sorry," Eve told her friends. "Ruining such a nice evening..."

"Don't be silly," Larry said. "I'm sure the restaurant has ice."

"No!" said Eve quickly. "I need to lie down and elevate it."

"That's right," said Steve. "Elevate it. High. Very high. I'll help you to the car."

"Oh, dinner would have been so much fun," Mary said sadly.

For an instant, Eve felt bad. Until Mary added, "Little Jerry will be so disappointed."

Steve and Eve shrugged apologetically, then Steve put Eve's arm over his shoulder, grabbed her waist, and helped her limp off.

"Sorry, you guys," Eve called back over her shoulder.

"Feel better," said Larry.

As soon as they rounded the corner, Eve removed her arm from around Steve's shoulder and they hurried toward their car.

"Where should we eat?" Steve asked.

"Someplace nice. With no children's menu."

"The Oak Room's not far."

"Isn't that a little pricey?"

"Yes, it is," Steve said, patting his wallet. "But you're in luck, ma'am. You're with a guy who has a *dode* card."

As they drove to the restaurant, Steve and Eve vowed that, when they became grandparents, they'd never be like Jerry and Mary. They talked about what being a grandparent can do to a person, then these two regular church-goers mused about how thick the Bible might have been if Jesus had had grandparents…

While walking down a village street one day, Jesus' grandparents run into a man they know.

"Hey, did you hear about what our grandson did?" the grandfather asks the man.

"You mean with the loaves and the fishes?" the man says, eager to make a hasty exit having already heard the story countless times.

"No, we're talking about what he did *yesterday*," explains the grandmother. "He walked on water."

"Walked?" the grandfather says, topping her. "He *ran*. Fastest time ever across the Sea of Galilee. By ten minutes!"

"And not only that," the grandmother continues. "He did it carrying those twelve friends of his on his back!" Then, with a caution particular to grandmothers, she adds, "Although I gotta tell you, that Judas guy looks a little shifty to me."

Later, after Steve and Eve had arrived at the Oak Room, Steve's cell phone rang. Caller ID showed that it was Larry calling.

Steve stepped into the foyer before answering.

"Hey, Steve," said Larry. "How's Eve doing?"

"Better, I think," said Steve.

"So the ice helped?" Larry wanted to know.

Steve looked toward their table, where Eve was enjoying a margarita on the rocks.

"Definitely," he said.

Then Steve heard some commotion coming over the phone.

"Oops, gotta go," said Larry with amusement. "Little Jer spilled a full water pitcher all over the table. I'm telling you … the kid is strong!"

Later during dinner, Steve and Eve received another phone call. This time it was from their daughter, with some very exciting news.

Her iguana laid eggs.

Steve and Eve were going to be grandparents!

ALL VEHICLES MUST STOP
"Hope your ears are clean!"

FIFTEEN

THE BEAUTY OF BELIEF

Once you've accepted that you're actually old enough to be a grandfather, it's normal to feel proud about your little accomplishments, like leaving the house three consecutive days without forgetting to zip your pants. But if you are still not entirely comfortable with your new status, I should mention an additional bonus that goes with the position.

Unlike your *children*, who wouldn't believe a thing you told them—and probably won't until they've experienced years of parenthood for themselves—your *grandchildren* will accept as gospel truth everything their grandfather says. And not only will they believe everything you tell them—no matter how ridiculous—they will also remember it. And they will remember it far longer than you will.

To support this theory, I offer two true stories from my own life. The first I experienced as a seven-year-old grandson. The second occurred when I had been a grandfather for seven years.

1. The distance from Los Angeles to Las Vegas is approximately 300 miles, and in 1954, the drive took a little over six hours in my parents' 1949 Buick Special. I was seven years old the first time I was allowed to go along to Vegas with them and my grandparents on what would be a weekend of gambling for them and non-stop swimming for me,

supervised by my grandmother. I had just finished second grade, where I discovered that reading came very easily to me, even the big words. Of course, I didn't choose to waste this talent on things like textbooks or encyclopedias, so on this trip I decided to read every road sign along the way. And I wouldn't just read them quietly to myself; I'd announce them to my parents and grandparents so they could also enjoy my special gift of incredible literacy. It would be a spelling bee on wheels!

"Motel Next Exit!" I bellowed, as though I was heralding the arrival of the queen at Buckingham Palace.

And less than a minute later, when I shouted "Barstow, 11 Miles," I suspected that I might have a future as a railroad conductor.

After about four hours of this, my father strongly suggested that I take a nap. I told him I wasn't tired, and spotted another sign up ahead.

"Next Gas, 42 Miles," I screeched, looking at my mother for approval. Instead, she closed her eyes and began massaging her temples. I assumed her headache was caused by my father, who insisted on driving with opened windows instead of using the air conditioner, worried that the car would overheat in the middle of the desert.

When I spotted an approaching series of Burma Shave signs, my father turned up the AM radio to a Bing Crosby song. My grandparents sat in the back, smiling, which I took as a mark of their appreciation for their oldest grandson's spectacular reading talent.

After two days of swimming in an over-chlorinated pool and catching a painful case of red-eye, it was time to head home again. I made sure I got plenty of rest before we hit the road, as there was no telling how many signs would need reading on the return trip.

But much to my disappointment, the signs on the way home were no more than mirror images of those on the first leg of our trip. Oh, I still read each one at the top of my voice; but the sense of newness, of challenge, was gone.

But then I saw a sign that I hadn't seen on the way to Las Vegas. And it had a big word on it … so I sounded it out in my head before I went public with it.

"In-speck-shun Stay-shun," I said. "Three Miles Ahead."

"That's right," said my grandfather. "Good reading."

"Thanks," I said. "But what do they inspect at the inspection station?"

Because it was my first trip, I didn't know that everyone driving from Las Vegas to Los Angeles is required to stop at an agricultural inspection station run by the State of California. Its mission is to prohibit plants, fruits, or shrubs that might bear insects from entering California from out-of-state. This inspection station still exists today, and if you have such a plant in your car, it will be politely confiscated by an agent of the California Department of Agriculture, who wears a uniform similar to that of a state trooper, complete with shiny badge and stiff broad-brimmed hat.

"They inspect your ears," my grandfather told me.

"My ears? Why would anyone want to inspect my ears?" I asked, not catching the amused reactions of the others in the car.

"Because," my grandfather said with great seriousness, "they want to make sure you're not bringing back any dirt in your ears from Las Vegas. Las Vegas has dirt that's very … dirty."

"Really?"

"Yessirree, Bob," Grandpa said. "I hope your ears are clean. Wouldn't want them to have to keep you there."

"Keep me?" I gulped.

"Yeah. Anyone whose ears aren't clean they make stay there and wash with special California ear cleaner. Then when they get enough of 'em, they put 'em on a bus and send 'em home."

"You mean someone with dirty ears has to stay out here? Overnight?"

"Overnight? Judas Priest, it could be a week before they get enough folks to fill the bus."

Grandpa said something else, but I couldn't hear him because I was busy scrubbing my ears with some saliva that I had deposited on the tail of my T-shirt, using it as a washcloth. And by the time we pulled into the inspection station, my ears were redder than if I'd gone ten rounds with Floyd Patterson.

As the inspector approached our car, my father got out and spoke to him for a moment. Then they went to the back of the car and opened the trunk. I didn't dare turn around to look; I was sitting between my grandparents, ramrod straight in my seat, hoping and praying that the inspector would think I was a statue whose ears didn't need checking.

When the trunk closed, the inspector began walking around the car and—without a word—he looked into my mother's ears, then my grandmother's, and finally my grandfather's. Apparently their ears all passed muster.

Then he motioned to me. "Okay, young man, step out of the car, please."

What? Why me? My ears couldn't be as dirty as everyone else's. I remembered that no more than a month before, I'd seen my grandma Q-tip out a chunk of earwax the size of a Hanukkah candle.

As I climbed over my grandfather and stood on the sweltering pavement, the inspector removed a small pocket flashlight and checked my right ear.

"Mmm, mmm..." was all he said. I took that as a bad sign. My ear probably had more wax than a beehive.

Then he shone his flashlight into my left ear.

"Oh, boy..." he muttered. Hearing this, I looked around to see where I'd be sleeping and wondered if coyotes and wolves would attack boys with dirty ears.

He stuck his flashlight back in his pocket and stared at me, deciding how to break the bad news.

But before he could speak, I heard my grandfather's voice.

"Officer, I'm the boy's grandfather and a veteran of the Spanish-American War," he said, getting out of the car. "First Boatswain's Mate, Pacific Fleet, Battle of Manila Bay," he explained, flashing his Navy tattoo of a dragon with an anchor in its mouth. "I know his ears are probably below standards, but he's a fine young man and an excellent reader, and I'd consider it a favor—one military man to another—if you'd let him come home with us today."

The inspector considered this for what seemed to be an hour, then looked to my grandfather. "It's a pleasure to meet you, sir," said the inspector. "And I'd be honored to do a favor for such a patriot as yourself."

I finally took a breath. The inspector crouched so he could speak to me face to face, ear to ear.

"You've got a fine grandfather, son. Now go on home and keep those ears clean."

"Yessir!" I said gratefully.

I had always loved my grandfather immensely, but never more than at that moment.

I climbed back into the car and we drove off into the sunset. I don't remember if I read any more signs the rest of the way. But I do remember promising myself that I would never drive from Las Vegas to Los Angeles again. And if I ever *had* to do it, I would leave my ears at home.

Nine summers later, when I wise old teenager of sixteen, my friend, Floyd, returned from a three-week vacation with his parents touring the West in a motor home. We sat at our kitchen table as Floyd told me about his travels while my mother washed breakfast dishes at the sink. Floyd didn't enjoy the trip at all, feeling that three weeks is entirely too long to spend with your parents; but he admitted that he did have fun when they stopped in Las Vegas on the way home. My still-red ears perked up when I heard this.

"Las Vegas? You *drove* home from Las Vegas?" I asked.

Floyd nodded, puzzled by my agitation.

"Did they check your ears?" I demanded.

Floyd didn't know what to make of my idiotic question. It was as if he had just told me he had won a million dollars and I answered him with, "Did you order the pot roast, Mrs. Hastings?"

At the sink, my mother started coughing and her shoulders began shaking. From behind, it seemed she was having some type of spasm.

"You okay, Mom?"

For some reason, my mother wasn't able to speak. But she did nod her head and hold up her hand, letting me know she was okay. Why she couldn't look at me, I had no idea.

Meanwhile, Floyd was still trying to make some sense of my question. "My ears? What the hell are you talking about?"

"When you drive home from Vegas, they check your ears for dirt," I explained. Then, as Floyd stared at me blankly, I suspected that maybe his ears were so dirty that his parents hid him under a bed in their rented motor home to avoid detection.

"There's this mean-looking police guy in a big hat, and..."

"Michael, could I speak to you for a moment please?" my mother asked, as she turned to me and wiped her eyes.

"*Michael*"? This must be something serious. She probably wanted to tell me she didn't approve of Floyd using words like *hell* in our house.

She took me into the next room and explained the truth about the inspection station. She would have told me years ago, but she'd forgotten all about it. Apparently everyone had. Except me.

My grandfather had lied to me.

"He didn't lie," she said. "He was just having fun with you. You were always his favorite. And I'm sure he'd tell you so if he were still with us today."

After I thought about it for a minute, I couldn't help smiling. Checking my ears for dirt? In the middle of the desert? How could I have believed such a thing? And how could I have continued believing it?

Because my grandpa told me, that's why.

2. More than forty-five years later, our seven-year-old granddaughter was swimming in the pool as my friend, Ray, and I look on.

"Buh-Buh, look!" she insisted before each belly flop off the board. And when she'd surface, she'd ask, "Was that a good one?"

"Excellent!" I told her. "Best dive I ever saw!"

And this went on for the next 229 dives over twelve minutes.

Finally, Ray called to her, "Can you do a swan dive?"

"What's that?" she asked.

Ray, wearing jeans and a long sleeve shirt, stood on the patio and demonstrated, spreading his arms wide and sticking out his chest. You need to know that Ray is also known as Big Play Ray. This is because Ray, quite simply, is a big guy. And although he has no grandchildren of his own, Ray thoroughly enjoys being around kids almost as much as they enjoy him. I think this is because Ray—as a successful working actor for over forty years—still has a healthy amount of child living within.

When my granddaughter saw Ray's detailed, over-the-top depiction of a perfect swan dive, she was awestruck.

"Were you a diver?" she asked with reverence.

Asking Big Play Ray if he was ever a diver is like asking Richard Simmons if he was ever a Green Bay Packer.

"A diver?" I repeated. "Have you ever heard of the Olympics?" I asked my granddaughter.

"You mean the ones with Mia Hamm?" she answered immediately.

"That's right. Well, Big Play Ray was an Olympic diver in 1957." Then I turned to Ray. "What was that specialty dive you were famous for?" I asked.

Seeing that he had a rapt audience in my granddaughter, Ray the Actor took over to create Ray the Olympic Diver. "Aw, I really don't like to brag about it, but it was a triple three-and-a-half corkscrew with two twists and a flying kayak!" he said modestly.

And then, with his trademark perfect timing, he whirled and contorted to demonstrate his signature dive, and then sat down to let my granddaughter absorb it. She stared at him admiringly for a moment, and then went back to her belly flops. And that was that.

But as it turned out, that wasn't even close to that.

Four years later, this same wonderful granddaughter was now in fifth grade. One night our phone rang and I answered.

"Hi, Buh-Buh," she said.

"Hey, darlin'. How are you?"

"Okay, I guess. I have to write a paper on the most famous person I know."

Wow, what flattery. There's no better feeling than being famous in your grandchild's eyes. Because if you're famous in your *children*'s eyes, it can be very expensive.

"Sure, honey, what do you want to know?"

"Your friend Big Play Ray's phone number," she said. "I'll be the only one in my class who knows a man who dove in the Olympics. Even if he is old."

"Ray?" I stammered? "The Olympics?" What was she talking about?

"Yes. Remember when I was swimming at your house and you told me about his special dive? A kayak or something?"

Then it hit me. What had I done? For a moment, I saw my beautiful granddaughter standing in the desert with a flashlight in her ear.

"Oh, right, the kayak ... Listen, honey, about Ray..." I quickly ran through a number of explanations in my head: "Ray can't talk; he lost his voice." "Ray's phone is broken." "Ray doesn't have a phone since he moved into a teepee." But I knew that would only make things worse.

"Maybe you could think of someone else to write about," I suggested.

"Like who?"

"Well ... like me."

"Buh-Buh, you're not famous. You're a writer." Hearing her thoughts on writers, I had a horrible thought: Could my granddaughter grow up to be a Hollywood producer?

"Now can I please have Ray's phone number?"

The truth would be hard, but I knew what I had to do.

"Honey, about Ray ... He never..."

That's when I heard her "call waiting" beep.

"Hold on, Buh-Buh," she said.

As I waited, I hoped that someday she'd find it in her heart to trust her grandpa again.

She came back on the line. "Never mind, Buh-Buh," she said.

"Pardon?"

"Big Play Ray. I don't need to talk to him anymore."

"Why not?"

"There was a man on the news tonight and his pig had babies. And one of the baby pigs has two heads!"

"And?" I asked.

"And my friend Ashley. That's her Uncle Leroy! And she doesn't go to my school, so I'm going to write about him!"

"Wow," I said with no small mount of relief. "That's a great idea."

"Yeah. What were you going to tell me about Ray?"

"Pardon?"

"You said, 'Ray never...' Ray never what?"

"Oh, that. Ray never ... Ray never is home at this time anyhow. He's out giving diving lessons."

"Oh. Well, bye, Buh-Buh. I love you."

"Love you too, sweetie. Bye."

And that night before I went to sleep, I kissed Jill good-night.

Then I thanked the Lord for friends like Ray and two-headed pigs.

SIXTEEN

THE FIVE COMMANDMENTS FOR GRANDFATHERS

Actually, there are *Ten* Commandments for grandfathers, but we'll only discuss the most important five, because now that you're of grandfather age, the last thing you need is more stuff to keep track of. Like me, I'm sure your mind is already fully occupied trying to remember things like which of those two numbers represents your *good* cholesterol, your bank-assigned PIN number, and where you parked your car at the mall.

This last example requires that I tell you a story before continuing with the Commandments. This story is true, and is one I've never told before. So if you promise not to relay it to my wife, this is a perfect time to get it off my sagging, grey-haired chest.

One day not long ago, I came out of the mall to discover that my car was not where I remembered parking it. After searching the parking structure for over an hour and still finding no trace of it, I finally had to accept the sad probability that my beloved BMW had been stolen. I called the police, who arrived quickly and began taking a crime report. As the officer transcribed my information onto a form, she asked if I happened to know the car's Vehicle Identification Number. When I told her that I could barely remember the

license number, she asked for my key ring—explaining that some manufacturers also engrave the VIN on the ignition key. When I handed her my keys, she studied them closely. Then she did something puzzling. She shot me a pitiful look and began shaking her head. I asked if there was a problem and, as politely as she could, she pointed out that the ignition key did not read "BMW." Instead, it read "JEEP." Examining the key, I felt my face grow flushed with embarrassment as I suddenly remembered one important piece of the puzzle. Jill had swapped cars with me that morning, saying that the BMW would be more comfortable for her to drive "the girls" to lunch in. I had driven her car to the mall.

I apologized to the officer for wasting her time and she left without giving me a lecture. She probably figured that no matter what she told me, I'd forget by the time I got home.

There was a silver lining, though. After the officer left, I turned to see Jill's white Jeep parked a mere two rows away. So I suppose one could argue that—subconsciously at least—I did not forget where I parked my car. I just forgot what car it was that I parked.

Now, let's get back to the Grandfatherhood Commandments. Though there is no fine or jail time for disobeying them, you should be aware that a violation can result in the revocation of your AARP benefits card.

I. THOU SHALT REMEMBER THINE AGE

What grandchildren expect from a grandfather is his undying love, his tender guidance, and his frequent disbursements of cash. What they don't want is someone who will ridicule their musical choices, urge them to do better in sports, and generally meddle in their lives.

For that, they have parents.

And, of course, their other grandfathers.

And although it's difficult for us accept the limitations of age, accept them we must. Do not be fooled by your deluded grandfather friend who proclaims that "Having a grandchild makes me feel young again!" If he feels so darned young, why does he need electric hedge clippers to trim his toenails?

The truth is that you are not young, and pretending that you are can have dire consequences. For example, let's say you have a twelve-year-old grandson who is a star baseball player. One day while you are visiting, he hands you a padded mitt and asks if you would catch him while he practices his pitching. He specifically asks *you* because you've told him of your baseball exploits when you were his age and, as we've already seen, grandchildren believe everything their grandfathers tell them.

It is now that you wish you hadn't embellished your athletic achievements. Although you *did* play baseball when you were a boy, the truth is that you spent most of your spare time in accordion lessons and collecting stamps, and were certainly not the All-Star you claimed to be. In fact, you played only two years—when you were six and seven—because your parents thought it would be a positive experience. And to say you "weren't very good" is like saying Billy Barty "wasn't very tall."

In fact, the only positive experience of your short baseball career was that both years, you had the same nice coach who gave every player a trophy designated especially for him at the end of each season. Your first year, your coach named you the team's "Most Valuable Listener." Your second and final year, you were rewarded as the "Most Improved Foul Ball Retriever."

But although your hands-on baseball experience is limited, you know enough to realize that your grandson is very talented, because you've been to a few of his games and have seen that he throws the ball hard. Very hard.

It's now that you have a difficult decision to make. If you choose to nurture your deluded self-image and perpetuate your hollow boasts, you will have to catch your grandson. And even though you recently had LASIK surgery, you know that your eyes are not keen enough to catch a ball coming at you as fast as your grandson can throw it. After all, when your wife gently lobbed you the car keys last week, they caromed off your forehead.

And since your grandson mentioned nothing about a catcher's mask, you need to calculate the price of protecting your ego versus the cost of replacing the bridgework you're still paying for.

And because he's only twelve, your grandson probably doesn't have pinpoint control. You've never owned a protective cup before, so you must also decide whether you want to risk experiencing the same breathtaking pain you endured immediately after your double-hernia surgery.

"You know what, Chuck, that's not going to work," you say.

"Why not, Poppo?" he asks.

"Well, because I'm too old. My eyes aren't that great and my reflexes are shot. Plus I never was really very good at baseball when I was a kid. In fact, I stunk."

"But you said..."

"I know what I said. But I only told you that to impress you. Sorry."

What are you saying?! The only way you could make a confession like that would be if you were on your death bed. So you force a smile, take the mitt, and suspect that pretty soon you will be.

II. THOU SHALT NOT COMPETE WITH THE OTHER GRANDPAS

Although it's only natural for you to want to be your grandchild's favorite, you are forbidden to use dirty tricks to gain unfair advantage. Although this Commandment is general in scope, grandfatherhood scholars have cited several specifics that are forbidden.

a) Off-handedly referring to your grandchild's other grandfather(s) in unflattering terms like "Grandpa Nose Wart," "Grandpa Out of a Job Again," or "Grandpa Rehab."
b) Purposely excluding the other grandpas from family events. For example, it is unacceptable to host a "spontaneous" barbecue to celebrate your grandson's first time wearing "big-boy pants" without inviting your counterpart and then telling your grandson, "Your other grandpa would have been here, but it was out of range for the electronic monitoring device he has to wear ever since he … Oh, never mind."
c) Trying to make the other grandpa's assets seem like liabilities, in spite of him being a handsome, self-made millionaire with a fleet of private jets and homes in New York, London, and Tahiti. And even though he donated his most recent seven-figure bonus to a charity he let *you* select, and spends his weekends with his seven children and wife of thirty-six years building homes for the needy, you should not try to discredit him. And just because he has recently become one

of the most popular male underwear models in the world while being two years older than you, it does not entitle you to … Aw, hell, *these* Commandments aren't written in stone! Torpedo the pretty boy!

III. THOU SHALT ADORN THY WAIST WITH NOTHING OTHER THAN A BELT

This is universal in nature and has no exceptions, regardless of race, creed or level of fitness. And while the reason for this Commandment should be obvious to any grandfather-aged man, there are an overwhelming number of you out there who insist on breaking the Third Commandment. I know this because I have seen you.

Simply stated, this Commandment prohibits older men from going out in public wearing what is known as a "fanny pack." There are numerous reasons for this, but we only need discuss a few.

First, to wear a fanny pack, one must still own a fanny. And because most grandfathers' fannies disappeared years ago, a fanny pack will draw attention to this loss, thus making the matching shorts/shirt ensemble that your wife bought you look even goofier than it already does.

"Look at that old man wearing a fanny pack," a younger person might say to her friend as they're caught in the logjam you've created by trundling your way down the middle of the sidewalk on a balmy, sunny day.

"I see," says her friend. "I wonder what's holding it up in back? The man has absolutely no fanny!"

"You're right about that," says the first girl with a sympathetic giggle. "No, wait, I think I see it!" she says as they hop through some ivy to pass you. "I believe his fanny has moved from his rear to his front!"

Fanny packs are perfectly acceptable for young people who roller skate, for old women who collect things, and for tourists from Eastern Europe and Ohio. If you're in none of these categories, here is a way for you to determine whether you should wear one of these annoying accoutrements: If your navel used to point due west but now points south or southwest, lose the fanny pack.

Going "packless" should not be at all difficult, since you have already spent most of your life not wearing one. If pockets were good enough for over fifty years, what makes you think you suddenly need a fanny pack? In reality, the older you get, the fewer things you need to carry with you. No business cards or appointment calendars; and because you no longer get job performance bonuses, your wallet is now a lot thinner and fits into your rear pants without hurting your fanny, even if you still had one.

The final reason grandfathers are forbidden to wear fanny packs is perhaps the most important: As men get older, they become more forgetful. This can result in a grandfather going to a restaurant with his fanny pack, removing it while he eats, then forgetfully leaving it behind. Last year, in fact, there were over five thousand reported cases of absent-minded older men leaving restaurants without their fanny packs—and their wallets. But the number of lost wallets is significantly smaller for men who choose to keep them in their trouser pockets. In fact, over the past two years, there was only *one* report of a grandpa leaving an establishment without his pants. And that was because of an incident involving his grandson's bachelor party.

In addition to fanny packs, this Commandment also prohibits older men from wearing one of those mesh waistband devices for holding bottled water. At your age, you have enough trouble holding the water you already have in you, so why tempt fate by drinking more?

Note that this Commandment does not apply to tool belts for those of you who are professional tradesmen, artisans, or craftsmen. Because if you are any of these, your grandchildren are likely very proud of you and will invite you to speak at their school to tell their class about all the wonderful things you've built.

If, however, you are a recently-retired insurance salesman and your entire tool collection consists of a hammer, two screwdrivers, and a can of WD-40, you are not allowed to wear a tool belt—or even buy one—even though you have plenty of time on your hands and just graduated at the top of your class from a two-day Home Depot course on "How to Add a Second Story to Your Home."

There is also a corollary to this Commandment which prohibits a grandfather from wearing his baseball cap backwards unless, at the age of sixty-seven, he is still a full-time major league catcher.

IV. THOU SHALT NOT SHOW FAVORITISM

Although it goes without saying that you love every one of your grandchildren, you need to understand the difference between the words "love" and "prefer." For example, while you may *love* steak, you may *prefer* a rib-eye. This is not to diminish your deep feelings for the T-bone, the New York strip, or even the flank steak. You truly care for all of them, and would defend them against anyone who said anything bad about them, including your mortician.

The same applies to your grandchildren. You *love* them all unconditionally, but you *prefer* the six-year-old granddaughter who tells you that she wants to marry a handsome, funny, smart man just like you. She is your Rib-Eye, while your fourteen-year-old grandson who never speaks and tromps around the mall with his baggy pants belted three inches above his knees is your Flank Steak.

But while your love for all your grandchildren is permanent, it is not unusual for your preferences to vary. This change usually results from events that come at you without warning—like your fourteen-year-old, non-speaking, underwear-showing Flank Steak calling you out of the blue and asking if you could teach him how to play cribbage.

When he arrives the next day, you wonder how he is able to walk with his pants like that. His low belt makes him take short, quick steps, which would be fine if he were in training to become a geisha girl. You also wonder what brought on his sudden interest in cribbage, a card game that's not at all popular among young people, and one that you learned from your grandfather.

When you ask him, he reminds you about his volunteer work at a senior home that's part of his high school curriculum.

"I thought you were only required to do that last semester," you say.

"Uh-huh," he mumbles, then explains, "I'm kinda doin' it on my own this semester."

"You mean for no credit?"

"Yeah. See, there's this old guy, George, who lives there. No one ever visits him, and he likes to play cribbage, so I figured I'd learn how."

"I'd say George is a lucky man."

"He's a cool old dude. You know … Like you, Grandpa."

And that's how a Flank Steak becomes a Rib-Eye.

So there's really no way to avoid having a favorite, even though that favorite may change from time to time.

The trick—as the Fifth Commandment ordains—is to avoid showing it. You must treat every grandchild with the same amount of love and respect.

And if you think this is easy, talk to the grandparents of Jimmy and Billy Carter.

Or Bill and Roger Clinton.

Or any of the Baldwin Brothers.

Rib-Eyes and Flank Steaks.

V. THOU SHALT KNOW WHEN TO ZIP THY LIP

Today's young parents do things a lot differently than we did, and I often wonder if the part of the brain that governs common sense is somehow adversely affected by those who consume too many four-dollar lattes. For instance, many of today's parents actually believe they should try to *reason* with a three-year-old.

Consider:

2008: "I don't see why I have to go to bed now," the toddler shouts. "Give me one good reason!"

"Okay, sweetie, let's discuss it."

1980: "I don't see why I have to go to bed now! Give me one good reason!"

"Okay, sweetie. The reason is 'cause I said so! Nighty-night!"

But a grandfather needs to refrain from commenting on his children's parenting practices unless he's asked, which will never happen because our children think they have found the true path to proper parenting.

Just like we did.

But holding your tongue is not always easy. Imagine that you call your six-year-old grandson to find out what he'd like for his upcoming birthday. Your daughter answers.

"Hi, honey," you say. "Is little Roscoe home?"

"No, Daddy. He's at a play date."

"A what?"

"A play date," she repeats.

"What the hell's that?" you ask.

"He made a date to go play with his friend Barlow."

"Barlow? Isn't that the kid who lives right next door?"

"That's right."

"Are you telling me that Roscoe had to make a date just to go next door?"

"Daddy..." she says, sensing that you may be having trouble with this parenting concept.

What you want to say next is, "*Play date*? Are you kidding me? Why does he have to make a date to play? What happened to running next door and yelling, 'Hey, Barlow, wanna play?' Or is Barlow too busy heading up a multi-national corporation to be allowed to play without an appointment?" A play date! Who comes up with this stuff? You've never heard such a crock! What does your daughter call dinner at her house? A nourishment date?

But instead, you must use the wisdom of your age to bite your tongue.

"That's nice," you say sweetly. "Could you please have Roscoe call me when he gets home from his play date?"

"Sure, Daddy. He'll be back in an hour."

But two hours later, Roscoe still hasn't called, so you call him again. This time your son-in-law answers.

"Oh, hi, Jim," he says to you. "What's up?"

"Same ol', same ol'. Can I talk to Roscoe for a sec?"

"Uh, hold on," your son-in-law says uneasily. Then he covers the phone and you can tell he's having an exchange with your daughter. Finally, he comes back on the line.

"He, uh, he can't talk to you right now, Jim."

"Oh, I'm sorry. Are you eating dinner?"

"No. Roscoe's having a time-out."

"A time-out?" you ask.

"Yep," says your son-in-law.

"A time-out? You mean he was playing basketball or something?"

"No, Jim. Roscoe's having a *time-out*." This time, he says the word slowly, thinking that he may be talking too fast for someone your age.

"A time-out from what?"

"From everything. After he came home from his play date, he was a little too rambunctious, so Colleen gave him a time-out."

"You mean she sent him to his room?"

"No, to the living room sofa."

"Roscoe's on your living room sofa?"

"Uh-huh."

"Doing what?"

"Sitting."

"Just sitting?"

"That's right. That's what time-outs are for."

"For sitting?"

"And for thinking about what he did wrong and realizing that he's responsible for his actions, and that those actions have consequences."

"A six-year-old will get all that from sitting? Couldn't he read a book or something?"

"No, that would be rewarding him."

You realize that if you continue biting your tongue at this rate, it will have more holes in it than Phil Spector's alibi.

But again, you must take the high road.

"Okay," you sigh. And then you schedule a *phone date* with Roscoe just as soon as he finishes his time-out.

And don't think that your child's approach to parenting only evidences itself *after* the child is born.

Our friends Charlie and Cynthia got their first hint of today's New Age parenting several months before they became grandparents. Their daughter, Janice, was in the seventh month of her first pregnancy, and they were attending a baby shower for her in Northern California. Although Charlie has had a long and successful career as a television comedy writer, he's learned that telling people what he does for a living can sometimes be a mistake. Some will either respond with, "God, how can you write that stuff? Whatever happened to shows like *All in the Family*?" Others will say, "Comedy writer, eh? My Uncle Bert works at the DMV, and he has so many funny stories. I'll give him your number!"

"So, Mr. Smith," said the short, plump, plain-looking woman as she approached Charlie at the backyard shower. "Janice tells me you're a writer," she said with admiration.

Charlie nodded politely. At least his daughter still thought what he did was kind of cool.

"What do you write?"

"Television," he answered.

The disappointment in her eyes was immediate and profound. "Oh, I don't watch television," she sniffed. "Unless it's PBS, of course."

"Of course," Charlie sighed. Then he asked what she did for a living.

"I'm a doula," she said.

"A what?" Charlie blurted. Was she admitting to being a member of some kind of sleeper cell? He scanned her belt for explosives. She looked clean, although on closer inspection, Charlie thought he detected just a trace of a dark stubble.

"Doula. Three of us will be assisting Janice at childbirth to provide a tranquil and peaceful environment for her newborn to arrive and thrive."

It took Charlie a while to process this. His daughter ran a successful consulting company all by herself, yet she needed three women to help her have a baby? She already had an OB/GYN and pediatrician that she raved about, plus she and her husband had been attending birthing classes twice a week for over two months. Why did she need these women? What would they do? Wave pom-poms and cheer, "Go, Janice! Go Janice!"?

"You mean you're a midwife?" Charlie asked the woman.

When the young lady heard that, Charlie could tell he'd made a huge gaffe. It was as if he had just met Wolfgang Puck and said, "Oh, you're a fry cook." The pudgy doula nearly leapt out of her Birkenstocks and strangled him.

"Don't you know anything about having a baby these days?" she asked with clenched jaw.

"Not much," Charlie said. "Just what I see on PBS."

A few minutes later, when his wife came over to join him, Charlie was still flabbergasted. "Cynth, do you know that when Janice has her baby, she's gonna..."

"The doulas, right?" Cynthia asked, rolling her eyes. "I just heard."

"What is she thinking? When she was born, it was you and her doctors in there with her. She needs three women?"

"I don't get it, either," Cynthia said. "Janice said all her friends are using doulas these days. It's kind of a fad or something."

"Hula Hoops are a fad! Nehru jackets are a fad! Needing three midwives to have a baby isn't a fad. It's nuts!"

"Doulas," Cynthia corrected with an ironic smile.

"Okay, fine. Since you're so up on the subject, can you tell me the difference between a midwife and a doula?"

Cynthia thought about this for a moment, then said, "About fifty dollars an hour."

Charlie never said a word to his daughter about it, though. Even when he later overheard the non-television-watching doula in a heated discussion with her boyfriend—a Chinese herbalist who should know better than to wear a ponytail—about who would be the next person thrown off *Survivor.*

SEVENTEEN

WORKIN' THE PERKS

Not only is grandfatherhood wonderfully rewarding on a personal and emotional level, but you will discover that it also provides a number of benefits that you should take advantage of every chance you get. And as you gain experience as a grandfather you will undoubtedly discover more perks designed especially for you, but here are a couple of my favorites to get you started.

American Idle

Psychologists have long held that the act of singing can help relieve stress, ease tension, and cause you to make a fool of yourself in karaoke bars. What's more, one recent television commercial claims that frequent singing can add up to four years to your life. And when I heard a companion spot suggesting that everyday laughter can expand your life by up to *eight* years, I determined that if we all walked around singing "Weird Al" Yankovic songs, we could prolong our lives by *twelve* years! But we would probably not have many friends.

But whatever the numbers, it's universally agreed that singing is a healthy thing. However, a grandfather should be cautioned that—if he's in a public place and not accompanied by his grandchildren—he should not break into a

10 ITEMS
OR LESS

raucous rendition of "Louie, Louie" or any other song from his youth.

Let's say you're in line at the grocery store when an instrumental version of one of your favorite oldies begins playing in the background.

At first, you don't really pay attention because you're too busy trying to make sense of the stack of coupons your wife made you take before she allowed you leave the house. But as you check to make sure you have the right coupon for a $.75 discount on a 400-pound bag of sugar, you become subliminally aware of the music and, without really knowing it, begin singing along. Soon, you are disturbing people as far away as the produce section.

"*Monday, Monday,*" you sing. "*So good to me. Monday morning, it was all I hoped it would be.*" You think you're sounding so good that you wonder why Mama Cass didn't ask you to be the third Papa. "*Oh, Monday morning, Monday morning couldn't guarantee that Monday evening you would still be here with me. Monday, Monday...*"

Then you hear the twenty-two-year-old clerk clear her throat, and you look up to see you're holding up the line, and that people are glaring at you impatiently and wondering why the older man in the *Grandpa Rocks* sweatshirt is singing so loud.

It's then that you're hit with a hard lesson: If you're young and sing in line, people smile and tap their feet. But if you're older, they raise their eyebrows sympathetically, particularly if you forget the lyrics and have a bottle of wine in your shopping cart.

Those people don't understand that even though a man may be older, he still has plenty to sing about. Maybe he's happy because his blood pressure medication had come off patent and went generic. Or maybe the forty-five-year-old suck-up who took his job just got canned for having some strange pictures on his laptop. Or perhaps he found out that Sansabelt pants are making a comeback.

But whatever the reason for your singing, people are still likely to see you as nothing but a doddering old coot.

But if you're singing along to the market's muzak while holding your three-year-old granddaughter, people will no longer see you as an old man who likely wears his undershorts backwards and inside out. Instead, they will look at you with admiring smiles. Some of the women in line may even sigh.

"*He's so fine, doo-lang, doo-lang, doo-lang. Wish he were mine, doo-lang, doo-lang, doo-lang, doo-lang...*" you croon as your granddaughter giggles, staring at you with utter enjoyment.

"Oh, look at how that beautiful little girl loves her grandfather," one woman thinks.

"And he has a very nice voice. I'll bet she grows up to be the free-spirited type. Just like him," thinks another.

And just like that, you have gone from a doddering old coot to a free-spirited Tony Bennett.

And until she's about ten, your granddaughter will occasionally ask you, "Grandpa, can you sing that *doo-lang* song again?" And out of experience, you will answer, "Sure, honey. Just as soon as we get to the supermarket."

Comfort Clothing

It's a known fact that as men get older, we dress less for style and more for comfort. I think this is why Levi-Strauss developed jeans labeled "Relaxed Fit," which in clothes-design lingo, means "Pants for geezers who love Cold Stone Creamery ice cream and hot pastrami sandwiches."

And because we dress for comfort, every grandfather has a favorite "comfort combo"—an old shirt with a ragged collar, pants with a hole in both rear pockets, and penny loafers that haven't been resoled since the break-up of the Kingston Trio.

But as much as we love these outfits, our wives forbid us wear them anywhere we might be seen by other human beings. This includes taking out the trash, bringing in the morning paper, and even opening the door for the pizza delivery kid, whose idea of a nice shirt is any one that doesn't hide the tattoo on his sternum.

But one weekend when your wife is out of town visiting her sister, you're wearing your outfit and decide to go out for coffee, assuming that no one will pay any attention to what you're wearing.

But no sooner do you shuffle into your neighborhood donut shop than an older man spots you and whispers to his wife, "Look at those clothes! Isn't that Martha Ferkenberger's husband?"

You hear him quite clearly because when older people think they're whispering, they're actually speaking at a volume level that would drown out a Hoover industrial vacuum.

"Yes, it is," says his wife. "Poor Martha. I hear he hasn't been the same since he retired from the insurance company and bought a tool belt."

"And last week Jim saw him at Home Depot!" her husband tells her. "Something about adding a second story."

You pretend you didn't hear them and leave with your coffee. What you don't know is that, because of your outfit, they followed you to make sure you were able to find your way home before too many other people saw you dressed like that.

Now let's look at the same scenario, but this time, your grandchild is involved.

It's two weeks later, and your five year-old grandson is visiting. Once again, it's Saturday morning and you are wearing your comfort outfit. Your wife is out shopping with the child's mother and your credit card. They are shopping because your daughter is pregnant again, this time with a girl. They are giddy because "now we can buy some *really cute* baby clothes."

"Grandpa, do you have any donuts?" your grandson asks.

"No, Luke, I don't think we do."

But when you see his look of disappointment, you quickly say, "But I know where we can get some!"

This time, when you walk into the donut shop, no one seems to notice your outfit. Instead, all they see is your grandson holding your hand and looking up at you like you're the most wonderful human being in the world.

And when you say to the clerk, "Yessir, my grandson would like a glass of milk and two of your finest chocolate donuts, please," you hear a lady whisper to her friend. "Look at that man with his grandson. Isn't that cute?"

And her friend says, "It sure is. And look how he hurried out of the house without changing out of those old clothes, just so the little boy wouldn't have to wait for his donuts. He doesn't care how he looks. I love a man who's secure with himself."

And when your grandson finishes his donuts, he says, "Thank you, Grandpa," and gives you a big, wet, gooey, chocolaty kiss.

And those two women look at you and think, "What a wonderful grandpa!"

And you know what? They're right.

EIGHTEEN

THE GRAND(PA) FINALE

So you made it to "Grandpa." Or "Po-Po," or "Bappa," or whatever wonderfully goofy name your grandchild has lovingly bestowed on you. You've accepted that you're actually old enough to qualify for the position and hopefully you're embracing it, luxuriating in it, and looking forward to all the wonderful things that come with the title of Grandfather.

But remember that it also brings some responsibilities, especially if you are a full-time grandparent to your grandchild.

Life sometimes leads us down a road for which we have no map, and those of you who have taken your grandchildren into your home to raise and nurture deserve the utmost respect. What you are doing is a very difficult job, and probably not one you volunteered for. But your grandchildren need your guidance, love, discipline, and patience. And because you give it to them without question, you are heroes. And certainly your grandchildren know it.

★ ★ ★ ★ ★

It's important that grandfathers possess certain qualities, and I've learned from my grandchildren that one of them is what I call "pretendability."

My most recent example of this came while I was spending a quiet Sunday morning planted on my den

WINDEX

sofa, concentrating on the crossword puzzle, when my granddaughter Samantha approached. "All right, sir," she said to me politely. "Thank you for waiting. Jenny's ready to do your hair now."

Two questions immediately occurred to me: Who is Jenny, and what is it that she intends to do to my hair?

"Sam..." I said, wanting to finish the puzzle.

"Buh-Buh," she whispered sternly. "My name's not Sam; it's Heather. I own this hair place."

"Oh, I see," I said, realizing we were moving into make-believe. I also realized my crossword puzzling would have to wait.

"Well," I said to Samantha, "if you're Heather, who's Jenny?"

"My best hair stylist. She's right over there."

Samantha (Heather) pointed to her three-year-old sister, Alexandra (Jenny), who was holding a hair brush from her Dallas Cowboys Cheerleader Barbie set and a spray bottle of Windex. I could guess what she intended to do with the brush, but the Windex puzzled me. Maybe she thought my hair needed a good industrial-strength washing.

Then Samantha called her little sister over. "Okay, Jenny. He's ready!"

As Alexandra ran over and prepared to attack my head, Samantha indicated that I should get off the sofa and sit on the floor so it would be easier for Jenny to work her magic, whatever it might be.

"How do you want your hair cut today, Buh-Buh?" Alexandra asked me, not realizing that she had just broken one of the cardinal rules of pretendability. As her grandfather, it was my job to set her straight.

"Who's Buh-Buh?" I asked her. "My name's Zack."

This puzzled the three-year-old, who hadn't yet amassed the pretending experience of her older sister.

"Hello, *Zack*," Samantha jumped in with a smile. A big wink was all the explanation Alex needed.

"Oooohhh!" she said, catching on. "So, Zack, how do you want me to fix your hair?" she asked.

"I think I'll have a double dockenfeller on top, with a bi-lateral klondiker on the sides."

"Okay," she said, not giving it another thought. "I did one of those yesterday." Then she prepared to spray Windex on my hair.

"Don't worry, Zack," Samantha confided. "It's only blue water. We put a melted popsicle in there." Then she handed Alexandra a handful of rubber bands.

Seven minutes and three gallons of sticky water later, Alex finished her work of art and handed me a mirror. My head was drenched, with rubber bands knotting my hair into about 325 stiff, dripping clumps.

"What do you think?" the girls asked.

What I thought was that I looked like Buckwheat in the episode of *The Little Rascals* where Spanky and he fell into a lake. But the girls thought I looked beautiful, and rewarded me with two delightful, mushy kisses on the cheek before they ran off to play "Starbucks Lady."

This reminds me of a story. Over the years, I've had the privilege to work with a number of wonderfully talented comedians. Among my short list of favorites is an intelligent, amazingly clever young man named Carlos Oscar, the father of two young girls. He tells a story about his younger daughter who received one of those Playskool "restaurant" sets for her birthday. As she was playing one day, Carlos passed by and she informed him that her restaurant was now a Starbucks.

"Would you like to order something, sir?" she asked.

"Yes, I would," said Carlos. "I'd like a Grande Nonfat Latte."

"Okay," his daughter replied, punching some buttons on her plastic cash register. "That will be twenty-three dollars and fifty cents."

"What?" Carlos asked. "That usually costs three dollars. Why so much?"

"Because," his daughter said without batting an eye, "my Starbucks is at the airport!"

Over the years, I've also been called upon to play characters like *Shane*, a third-grade student when Sydni was six and wanted to play "Miss Summers, School Teacher," and *Cody*, a restaurant customer who Samantha had a crush on when she pretended to be a waitress named Marsha.

And while pretendability is an important quality for grandfathers, perhaps even more important is that of wisdom. You must understand that since your grandchildren see you as the oldest person on the planet, they also expect you to be the smartest.

"Grandpa, how fast could *Tyrannosaurus rex* run?" your five-year-old grandson asks after watching a dinosaur video. By the look on his face, you can tell that he chose to ask you because you were probably once chased by one.

"That's a good question," you tell him. "Mr. Rex was fast. Very fast."

"Faster than a speeding bullet?" he asks.

"Apparently not, or he'd still be around," you say. This satisfies him for now; but that night you research everything you can find on the beast. You phone your grandson the next day, ready to present all the information you've gathered. He'll be thrilled.

"Twenty-eight miles per hour," you tell him.

"Huh?" he says.

"That's how fast a *Tyrannosaurus rex* could run. Twenty-eight miles an hour."

Silence. A silence that tells you he has no idea what you're talking about, and that yesterday's conversation has gone to that mysterious place where all forgotten conversations with five-year-olds disappear.

Then he speaks. "Okay, Grandpa. Whatever. Bye." Then he drops the phone and scampers off to find his mother so maybe she can make some sense of what you were talking about.

But as your grandchildren get older, you'll find that their questions will be a bit more probing. And they still believe that you do have the answers. Or perhaps they just *want* to believe it.

Recently, my oldest granddaughter and I went out to lunch together. Sitting across from her, I found it hard to believe that—seemingly overnight—she had grown from the baby I held just after she was born into a beautiful and intelligent thirteen-year-old young lady whose days of playing "school teacher" were well behind her. When Sydni finished telling me about a boy in her class whose grandmother had just died, she thought for a moment, then asked me, "Buh-Buh, do you believe there's a heaven?"

In truth, with all the seeming madness in today's world, I sometimes wonder. But that discussion was for another day. Like when she gets her Doctorate in Philosophy.

"Yeah, I do think there is," I told her. "What about you?"

"Well, I *want* to," she said.

So I asked her what she thought heaven was like.

"Well, I think it's where you go when you die and everyone you ever loved in your whole life is there waiting for you. Even Domino." (Their family Dalmatian had gone to the Big Ranch in the Sky several months earlier.) "And I think everyone's always happy, and no one has to be homeless and there aren't any wars. And Alexandra doesn't have cystic fibrosis anymore."

"Wow," I said honestly. "That's exactly what I think heaven is like, too."

She was glad to hear this, but as she swirled her ice cream with her spoon, I sensed that there was something else she wanted to talk about. And whatever it was, she was giving it a lot of thought.

"Buh-Buh," she finally said, choosing her words carefully. "If you die before I do..."

"Yeah?" I asked.

"I mean, like waaaaaayyyy before I do..."

"Okay, Syd, I get the point," I said with a laugh.

"Okay. So, like, when I die and go to heaven, and you're already there, you'll remember me, won't you?"

Wow. So that was it.

"Sydni," I said, trying to keep my heart where it belonged, "I could never, ever forget someone as special as you."

"Oh, good," she said with a relieved sigh.

Then she offered me a bite of her strawberry sundae.

It tasted great.

And that was a very good grandfather day.

ACKNOWLEDGMENTS

Without the encouragement, advice, and mentoring of Daniel Lazar at the Writers House, this book would not exist. Thanks, Dan and Josh, for your patience and humor. Likewise, I am forever grateful to the good folks at Skyhorse, especially Mark Weinstein, for his belief in this project and for his incisive editing, done with a sharp, tasteful eye and fine humor. And for the amazing illustrations, thanks to the enormously talented Renee Reeser Zelnick.

Thank you, Mr. Bill Cosby—not only for the kindness of your words here, but for the gifts of laughter, intelligence and inspiration you continue giving people everywhere. And thanks for hiring me all those times, too.

To the extremely beautiful and beguiling Sydni, Samantha, Alexandra, and Claire for being wonderful muses and for providing an aging, goofy grandfather with the unbridled joy he needed for this project. Thanks for letting me tell people about you.

I'm particularly lucky to have a loyal squad of cheerleaders. Led by my ever-smiling Jill, they have been incredibly supportive, generous, and encouraging every step of the way. Ray and Marlene, Mady, Zip and Denise, Patti and Dave, you are the absolute best. Next round is on me. But don't hold me to that.

To Leroy and Carol, Tim and Cindy … thanks for sharing.

And finally, to John, Kevin, Rebecca, Ron, Dionn, Kevin, and Mischon, the parents of some wonderful grandchildren, both present and future. (Hint, hint … and you know who you are.)

ABOUT THE AUTHOR

Michael Milligan has been a working comedy writer for over thirty years, with credits including *Good Times, Maude, All in the Family, The Jeffersons,* and *Dear John*.

In *this* century, he's had the unique pleasure and good fortune to work with Mr. Bill Cosby on several projects, including *Here and Now* and Nickelodeon's *Fatherhood*. Series he's written have been acknowledged with Good Housekeeping's Award for Family Television, as well as awards for excellence from the NAACP, GLAAD, and the organizations Nosotros, Alma, and Imagen.

Michael lives with his wife, Jill, in Los Angeles, which is 316.5 miles and a five-hour drive from their grandchildren. Unless Jill drives, because he claims she can make it in four hours and thirty-seven minutes. And Michael tells us she has a distended bladder and two diplomas from traffic school to prove it.